ART CENTER COLLEGE OF DESIGN
Continental

D0468136

THE LOVE OF GYMNASTICS

THE LOVE OF GYMNASTICS

Edited by Jim Prestidge
Foreword by Nelli Kim

CRESCENT BOOKS

New York

First English edition published 1979 by Octopus Books
Limited, 59, Grosvenor Street, London W.1.

© MCMLXXIX Octopus Books Limited

Library of Congress Catalogue Card Number: 78-23647
This edition is published by Crescent Books,
a division of Crown Publishers, Inc.

Library of Congress Cataloging in Publication Data

Prestidge, Jim.
The Love of Gymnastics.

1. Gymnastics I. Title.
GV461. G65 1979 796.41 78-23647
ISBN 0-517-27340-3

Printed in Hong Kong

Contents

Additional text by David Brenner

Left
*The bravery and timing of one of France's
leading gymnasts, Henry Boerio, on the
high bar made spectators catch their
breath at the World championships for
which France played hosts at Strasbourg
in 1978.*

Half-title
*The elfin Olga Korbut in full flight and on
the way towards capturing all hearts at the
Olympic Games in Munich, in 1972. After
Olga, nothing in international gymnastics
was ever quite the same.*

Foreword

First, I would like to express my pleasure at being invited to write the foreword for this book. I am sure that enthusiasts all over the world will enjoy its illustrations and informative text. The 1980 Moscow Olympics should include some of the finest international gymnastics ever seen. Standards are improving so rapidly throughout the world, and there are now 12- and 13-year-old children performing exercises I could not have imagined when I was at that age. I will be 21 when the Olympics are held in my country, and I will have to compete not only against my rivals but against time itself if I am to succeed. To retain my position, I am having to constantly update my programme, making the task even more difficult. That is not only a challenge, but one of the great things about gymnastics today. It is never boring, either for the gymnast or the spectator, as there are always new ideas being developed.

Our Soviet teams should be strong for the Olympics. There are many young people in our country who are developing well. They will be especially keen to perform to the best of their ability in Moscow, as this is the first time that the Games have been held in the Soviet Union. I hope our friends and readers of this book will enjoy watching the Olympic Games on television. We are proud of the facilities we have provided for this occasion, and to be hosts to the world for the 1980 Olympics. It is our sincere wish that competitors and spectators alike will join us in Moscow with the true spirit of the Olympiad.

My fellow gymnasts and I are always impressed with the warm welcome we receive when visiting your country. I hope that the pages of this book will tell you more about our sport and provide you with a great deal of enjoyment.

Nelli Kim, Moscow 1979

7

The World of Gymnastics

From the Romans and the Greeks to the World

Gymnastics is a sport with a long and fascinating history. It takes in such diverse characters as a doctor of Roman times who "invented" the keep-fit class, a German secret agent, who could be legitimately called the real father of the sport as we know it today and two tiny teenage girls whose magnetism and ability brought the love of gymnastics to the world.

It is July 22, 1976. The scene is The Forum in Montreal, Canada. A world-record crowd for any gymnastic event of 18,000 enthusiasts is crammed into the auditorium to watch the individual apparatus events for women, the culmination of the gymnastic championships of the Montreal Olympic Games.

And there, unfolded before that intent and electrified audience, was a display of gymnastic skills unparalleled in the history of the sport. A tiny, dark-haired, serious little girl from Rumania, called Nadia Comaneci, not

Left
Rumania's extraordinarily gifted Nadia Comaneci, the overall women's champion at the 1976 Montreal Olympics, demonstrates one of her heart-stopping specialities – the Radochla somersault on the asymmetric bars

15 until the following November, was about to achieve perfection . . . not just once, but seven times, scoring an astounding 10 out of 10 in seven of the team and individual exercises.

Our story back-tracks four years, to another Olympic scene, the Munich *Sporthalle*, where another charismatic waif-like figure is about to captivate the audience and the watching world on television with a unique blend of uninhibited ability and elfin charm. The girl this time is a Russian, Olga Korbut. And she was the girl who transformed gymnastics almost single-handed from a comparatively minority sport into the world-wide phenomenon it has now become.

A back somersault on a beam just 4in. wide, a dazzling display of bar and floor exercises performed with a grin and completed with an impudent grace, endeared Olga to the world. After Olga nothing would ever be quite the same again . . .

Olga wrote her own particular page later on in the long and fascinating story of gymnastics — a story which starts before the birth of Christ back in Ancient Greek and Roman times.

The Greeks had, like so many civilisations before and since, learned how to enjoy their own particular pattern of physical play. They would wrestle, fight, climb ropes, throw weights and javelins, in fact take part in all manner of physical activity.

The Greeks very soon realised that none of these energetic skills could be performed with freedom while wearing the voluminous fashionable cloaks of the day. They simply retreated to the seclusion of the Palaestra, where, having shed their robes, they were free to pursue their gymnastics. Hence one definition of gymnastics: "To perform exercises whilst naked!"

The Palaestra was essentially the wrestling room and became the focal point of the men's daily recreation. Around and about the Palaestra would be numerous other rooms for other activities. Mats as we know them today were unknown, but the floors of the activity rooms would be covered with sand. There were also baths, changing rooms, lecture rooms and a place for relaxation and discussion after a hard session and the Gymnasium, this being the general name for the complex of buildings, became a Grecian version of a men's club.

It is not possible to establish precisely what form the gymnastics followed. The only records we have are the designs shown on ancient Greek pottery showing various examples of gymnasts jumping, rope climbing, running and, of course, wrestling. The word *gymnastics* came to be defined as any physical activity that was performed in the gymnasium.

The story of the growth of gymnastics now takes a giant jump from one civilisation to another.

The Romans who superseded the Greeks and in fact overlapped them, were able to copy and perpetuate their cultural ideals. But as the centuries went by, the Romans were unable to maintain the high moral code set by the Greeks and probably, partly because of this, the Roman empire and civilisation collapsed. Nevertheless, they made a lasting contribution to mankind and to our gymnastic history.

The Romans started with good intent and constructed fine buildings, the counterpart of what today we call sport or leisure centres. Such a centre was the Caracalla, erected by the Emperor of that name. This incredible building contained everything which we would consider essential in a gymnastics and recreation centre today. There were swimming pools; both remedial and for play, gymnasia massage rooms, club rooms and a library. It served the Romans for more than 400

years—until the decline of the empire.

The complex of buildings then stood neglected and partly in decay for centuries, right up until the Rome Olympic Games of 1960. It was then refurbished to become the venue for the Olympic gymnastic events. It is still in use today, providing facilities for opera productions and other spectacular events and entertainments. A power-

Above
Russia's Olga Korbut, who popularised world gymnastics.

Right
Nadia Comaneci, Korbut's successor in public affection, in action.

ful link with the past is preserved in this way, and it also serves as a tribute to the Romans who built it.

If the Caracalla gives us such a valuable insight into the past, so did a Roman doctor, called Claudius Galen. His writings have told us much about physical education of that time, as many of the other great Roman biographers did. Galen was, perhaps, the first of many learned men who have, across the ages, endeavored to elevate physical play into a scientific and meaningful way of life; into a form of education. Many others were to do so after him, but for much different motives . . .

As a doctor Galen studied medical gymnastics — what we today would call "therapeutics". Galen also advocated gymnastics for the masses and thus gave us another contemporary link with the past — keep-fit exercises. Above all, he believed gymnastics should be fun.

It is one of the extraordinary quirks of history that Galen's writings, like the caracalla, should be ignored throughout the Dark Ages of European culture, to be unearthed centuries later and used so efficiently.

Our story must now jump again, sweeping through and beyond the Dark Ages almost 1,500 years ago, to the 18th and 19th centuries. We are now in Germany, Denmark and Sweden, where gymnastics is born again and our first focus is on Germany, because it is here that the sport of gymnastics as we know it today first began to flourish anew. Two Germans more than any others, Guts Muths and Friedrich Ludwig Jahn, influenced the growth of gymnastics in Europe. Muths took much of his inspiration from Galen, whose writings were now being studied by many educationists of the 18th century. As a teacher he studied the works of Galen and used many of his principals. Later, Muths' book *Gymnastics for Youth* had a profound influence on the teaching of gymnastics in Europe.

But it was Jahn, born in 1778, who was the real "father" of modern gymnastics. He saw in the sport something entirely different from his contemporaries and predecessors. Unlike the others, he was not concerned with education, but as a fanatical patriot, was motivated by a strong desire to free Germany from the occupying Napoleonic forces. He started physical fitness classes for boys and young men, and built his first outdoor gymnastics centre in a park — the *Hasenheid* — in the outskirts of Berlin. This site was the first of many which were to spread not only through Germany, but eventually around the world; the *Turnverein* — the German gym club.

However, Jahn had many problems and spent most of his 74 years in conflict with authority. Jahn's patriotic zeal prompted him to devise a new name for gymnastics — he chose *Turnen*, a German word for which there is no simple translation. The nearest equivalent English word is "joust". During the next 50 years *turnen* grew to become a highly specialised and

Below
This detail from a Greek vase shows how early athletes competing in jumping events used to hold weights to achieve greater distances.

Above
Daring feats by acrobats in the Minoan culture of ancient Crete often involved somersaulting over the horns of a bull.

competitive sport.

Jahn's Swedish contemporary was Pehr Ling. He was to develop a form of gymnastics which more easily fitted the educational requirements of the time and did in fact become the basis of physical education throughout the world. And it is now clear that the sport of gymnastics was being welcomed in schools, both as an after-school activity and in some cases as part of the school physical education programme.

Jahn's outdoor gymnasium in the *Hasenheid*, drawings of which still exist, show what can only be described as a maze of masts, ladders, climbing frames, horizontal bars, ropes, pits and horses. The horses looked more like the real animal at that time, instead of the stylised wooden and leather obstacle with which we are so familiar in gymnasia today.

Jahn was obviously confused. He had no guidance about what he should do, or indeed, how he should do it. What he was seeking to achieve had never been tried before, and his gymnastic systems involved much more than simple body movements. He introduced apparatus, hence the strange scene at *Hasenheid*. He then experimented with various ideas, invented apparatus as and when he thought it desirable and his gymnasts would then devise exercises to perform on the equipment. The boys and young men who were trying to outwit each other began to think up complex skills and gradually began to compete against each other. From that moment, the sport of competitive gymnastics was born.

At first and for many years afterwards, each club had its own apparatus, and ideas. Some clubs had rules, whilst others had no rules at all! However, while all this was happening, Jahn was still unable to avoid involvement with the underground movement, trying to free Germany from the Napoleonic influence. Indeed, he was a German secret agent for four years. Eventually he was arrested, and during his imprisonment, all the gymnastic clubs he had inaugurated were closed by the police. Jahn spent the next six years under close arrest or in prison, and the ban on his *Turnvereinen* lasted for 22 years.

It was during these decades that the clubs, which were all patterned on the open air *Hasenheid*, went indoors to escape detection and continued their activities in secret.

"Underground" equipment had to be smaller, more compact and, as much as anything, suitable for stowing away in a great hurry! All these changes were to have far reaching and important effects upon the development of the sport which during the following 60 years would spread around the world. It is ironic to think that if the ban on Jahn's activities had not been imposed, gymnastics might never have gone indoors, and the sport as we know it today might never have got off the ground. Significant, too, was the fact that the persecution of the *Turn-vereinen* led to many people fleeing the country and emigrating to England and the United States of America.

In America, especially, they spread the *Turnverein* idea and many American gym clubs today still exist with the word "Turner" in their club name.

In England the immigrants' arrival led to the formation of the very successful German Gymnastic Club.

Between 1850 and 1900 nearly every European country and the U.S.A. experienced its gymnastic "invasion". The sport became very popular in Britain, in spite of strong competition from other national games such as football and cricket.

The British national body, the Amateur Gymnastics Association was formed in 1888, and soon after its inception women and girls began to show an interest in gymnastics. It was inevitable that women, too, should wish to use the same apparatus as that used by men. However, the men and boys of that time were quite aware of the physical strength and power required to master the skills they were attempting, and for many years there was strong criticism of women taking part in any sport, especially gymnastics. It was in fact condemned by many educationists as well as the medical profession of the day.

It was many years before it was considered safe or even respectable for women to participate in such robust physical exercise, and even then the breakthrough did not happen until the development of specialised women's apparatus and the big impact of the Russian women gymnasts in the 1952 Olympic Games. But the movement grew in strength over the next 20 years, and soon women and girls were performing not only with great skill but also with the charm and grace of ballet dancers. By the early 1970s they had overtaken the men in terms of world popularity, and youngsters like Korbut, Comaneci and Nelli Kim suddenly became household names. The criticisms of the Twenties, when a news columnist disparagingly called the British women's team "brazen hussies" was now long forgotten.

The story of gymnastics is now almost up to date, and is completed by the overwhelming influence the Olympic Games has had on the sport.

Above
Acrobats and tumblers were a popular source of entertainment throughout Europe in medieval times, with feats as spectacular as this dive through hoops being particularly appreciated.

Left
Bearing a more-than-passing resemblance to a present-day circus troupe, these Japanese gymnasts of the late 19th century entertain onlookers in a make-shift "arena".

Right
A stylised Victorian illustration depicting the masculine ideals of wrestling during the original Olympiads of ancient Greece.

The first Olympic era is supposed to have begun in 776 BC, at a time when Greek ideology was thriving. It lasted for many centuries, and during that time gymnastics, in all its many facets, developed. But as moral standards declined, and unhealthy commercialism crept into the Games, so they lost much of their dignity. Eventually, with the decline of the Greek civilisation, so too the first Olympic era came to an end.

The ancient Olympic Games stayed dead for more than 1,500 years until

Left
As yet, the gymnasts of China have not established themselves at World level, but the inherent grace and poise of the Chinese is amply demonstrated by Chu Cheng, caught here in mid-routine on a beam exercise.

the enthusiasm and dedication of a group of men, headed by the Frenchman Pierre de Coubertin, led to the revival of the modern Games. The first Olympic Congress of modern times met in the Spring of 1894 and resulted in Coubertin's lifelong dream coming true. Two years later, in 1896, the first Olympic Games of modern times took place in Athens. From then on, except for the war years, the Games have taken place regularly every four years, with the World Gymnastic Championships interspersed between them.

Previously, gymnastics had been a very haphazard activity, performed mainly for fun rather than as a competitive sport. The clubs which had mushroomed all over Europe and America had no common standards, apparatus, rules or even dress.

It was the Olympic Games movement which forced the governing bodies to rationalise and develop the sport. It also hastened the formation of an international body for gymnastics. At last the sport had outgrown its European roots and was approaching the time when it would become a world-wide activity.

Up to the end of the 19th century the development of gymnastics had been very much at the whim of each individual nation. Some were motivated by patriotism, some by physical education and others simply pursuing a form of leisure activity. It was not until an international control body was formed in 1881, the European Gymnastic Federation, that the sport began to follow any rational standardised pattern, and it took well over half a century before the sport reached the format which it follows today. It was under the European Federation that the first official international event took place in Brussels in 1901. Two years later, the first World Gymnastics Championships were held in Antwerp, and the four competing teams — France (116 points), Belgium (109 points), Luxembourg (101 points) and Holland (95.1 points) — performed on

parallel bars, horizontal bars, horse and rings. There was also a 150-metre race, a high jump and weight-lifting and a 40kg weight had to be lifted 20 times! Except for the war years, the new championships took place every four years.

It took some time for the confusion to be eliminated with the inclusion of other events, and in fact things, at first, got worse. In 1911, the fifth championships were held in Turin, and besides the gymnastic events, there was pole-vaulting, shot-putting, 100-metre sprints and rope-climbing.

In 1922, swimming had also been added as a compulsory event. The World Championships were beginning to assume the characteristics of the Olympic Games themselves. Indeed, the first World Gymnastics Championships after World War Two, in 1948, still included high jump, pole vault and 100 metres.

Six years later in Rome, the 1954 and 13th World Championships followed for the first time the classic gymnastic programme for men as we know it today — six compulsory and six voluntary exercises and the athletic events were withdrawn. Women had now entered the contest and their

programme of four compulsory and four voluntary exercises was also fixed.

This 13th championship was a giant step forward for world gymnastics; not only because it established competitive gymnastics in the form we know it today, but because of the entry into the field for the first time of the Soviet Union and Japan. It is difficult to imagine how these two countries, traditionally and geographically out of touch with the mainstream of European gymnastics, could bring so much quality and appeal to this centuries-old sport. At last, gymnastics with its Greek and Roman origins plus its many European influences of the past, was being acclaimed and performed by the world.

The impact made by the Soviet Union can be understood simply with a glance at the results sheet for the 1954 World Championships in Rome. In the individual classification 132 men took part and Soviet gymnasts participating took the first seven places. The Soviet women's squad performed just as brilliantly, coming first in both the combined exercises and team events. Since then, they have remained the undisputed overall leaders of the world of gymnastics although, in 1962 in Prague, the Japanese team took over the coveted first place from the Russian men. The period between those Russian and Japanese triumphs and now has offered us the most exciting and colourful period of the entire history of gymnastics and has culminated in the emergence of such great performers as Korbut, Comaneci Tourischeva and many others.

If 1954 was a vital turning point, then 1978 may well have been another. A few days before the Strasbourg championships began, the F.I.G. (Fédération Internationale de Gymnastique) Congress agreed to accept a new nation into its membership — China. The People's Republic of China had been a member 20 years previously, but only for a brief period, when for reasons of their own, they decided to withdraw. During their short period of membership, they had hauled them-

Left
Concentration is etched into the face of Japan's brilliant Eizo Kenmotsu as he competes in the vault during his overall silver medal-winning performance at the 1978 World Championships.

selves up to fourth place in the men's team event, and sixth place in the women's. Their welcome return to the world arena could have the same impact upon the sport as did Japan's and the U.S.S.R.'s 20 years ago. The skill of the Chinese as tumblers and acrobats is legendary, and those who have had the pleasure of seeing them, will remember vividly their ability to combine skill and elegance in a way few others can match.

The F.I.G. made some big decisions affecting the sport, in 1978. It decreed that the World Championships should take place every two years, the next being in December 1979. The reason it was brought forward a year was to avoid clashing with the 1980 Olympic Games in Moscow. Furthermore, the World Championships, now becoming a more frequent event, will provide a more convenient qualification competition for Olympic events. The reason this qualification has become necessary is because of the increasing number of participants taking part in each successive Olympiad. It has

Left
Hungary's Eva Kanyo, only 19th overall at the 1978 World Championships, nevertheless scored a magnificent 9.5 points for her beam exercise.

therefore become necessary to limit the number of teams taking part in the gymnastic events, and this can only be done by a process of elimination.

Only the first 12 teams of six men and women will qualify. Having established the first 12 qualifying countries in this way, countries placed in the 13th, 14th and 15th positions will *each* be permitted to include three individuals. The next three countries, that is those in the 16th, 17th and 18th positions will *each* be permitted to include two individuals.

This ruling, though essential, is certain to cause some distress to many gymnasts. This is, perhaps, one reason why many gymnasts prefer participation in the World Championships. To the gymnast, this is as important as the Olympics, and in many ways more enjoyable. The World Championships have become more than a trial of gymnastic prowess among the world's best competitors, but a family occasion and a reunion with friends from all over the world. Many competitors who first met at these championships some years ago, reflect upon their own achievements and watch with intense interest the performances of young gymnasts of today.

It was on an occasion such as this that the ideal setting was provided for the World Gymnastic Championships in Strasbourg 1978. The arena was set with the podium for the men's compulsory competition, with five pieces of apparatus surrounding the 12-metre square floor area. Upon these items, the men performed their exercises. The compulsory exercises are generally considered to be of less interest than the voluntary exercises, but this was not so in Strasbourg. The enthusiasm and exuberance of many of the lesser teams, showed their determination to impress judges and audience alike, proved a distinct compensation for their lack of skill. Within minutes of the start, Olympic and Soviet champion Nikolai Andrianov had fallen from the pommel horse. To follow this most unexpected occurrence, Vladimir Markelov, reigning European champion, made the same mistake. This was a major setback for the Russians, and three days later, we were to recall those two falls when we learned that Japan had retained their World team title by only 0.95 of a point.

The Japanese, always the big attraction at these events, were due to perform later on the evening of the first

Above
Eizo Kenmotsu on the parallel bars at the 1972 Munich Olympics. A bronze medallist in this event, he was also the combined exercises silver medallist.

Right
The Cuban Ortega performs on the pommel horse. Although not in the medals the Cubans give great enjoyment to audiences.

day. After the excitement of the morning, we expected a quieter afternoon, relaxing with the lesser teams. Much to our surprise, it was not the quiet afternoon we expected. The Cubans appeared looking more like the Harlem Globetrotters than a national gymnastic team. These huge men gave a display of vaulting and tumbling that was among the most interesting seen that day. While we watched the Cubans, we completely forgot about our future date with the Japanese that evening. The Japanese immaculate style and skills were well demonstrated two days later during the voluntary exercises, but the performance given by these big Cubans was remarkable.

The scoreboard shows:

RS ADRIN ... 3 0
AP KENMOTSU 58 0 0
AP KASAMATS 58 0 5
RS DITIATIN 57 9 5

Above

Against the brilliantly-lit backdrop of the electronic scoreboard, detailing the progress of competitors during the men's combined exercises at the 1978 World Championships, Hungary's Zoltan Magyar – primarily a pommel horse specialist – comes out of a dislocate during his routine on the rings.

When the Japanese arrived that evening, there was an atmosphere of anti-climax. The Japanese, as did the Russians, made their share of mistakes. They hold a position in gymnastics which is unique, and despite their lead over the Russian men, they display, even under intense pressure, a combination of modest charm, good humour and dignity. It is impossible not to be endeared by them. The Japanese team chosen for Strasbourg came as a shock to those who have followed their successes for a decade or more. They were, without doubt, the oldest gymnasts in the competition. Kenmotsu and Tsukahara had been in the Mexico Olympics exactly 10 years

before, and were thought to be retired. The others, Kasamatsu, Kajiyama, Shiraishi and Shimizu were all mature and experienced gymnasts. Could they hold out against the youth and power of Russia, East Germany and the U.S.A.?

The compulsory exercises had taken toll of novice and champion alike. That is precisely what they are intended to do — to discover the weaknesses, the Achilles heel of every gymnast. The Japanese, too, had their failures, and with all the smiles they could muster they could not hide the fact. At the end of the day, the commanding lead which we had all expected after a disastrous start by the Russians was less than three points. In third place was East

Germany, and fourth, the outstanding U.S.A. team.

Ever since the Americans first entered the championships in 1958, they have held respectable team positions around sixth and eighth places. They were never able to break through to the medal positions. After the compulsory exercises in Strasbourg, it seemed as though they were in a position to challenge the top three, if not as a team, at least with some individual medal chances. The British team's performance had been disappointing, as they struggled through those tantalising exercises. Only Ian Neale of the British team showed confidence and ability. Two days later he was to emerge as one of Britain's greatest ever gymnasts. His score after the 12 disciplines was 111.4 points out of a maximum 120 points. The second day was reserved for the compulsory exercises for women.

Two of the greatest gymnasts of this decade had now passed into retirement, Ludmila Tourischeva — to marry Olympic sprinter Valery Borzov and have a child — and Olga Korbut. During the past eight years they had won the following medals in World and Olympic competitions:
Tourischeva:
10 gold, five silver, four bronze;
Korbut:
five gold, six silver, one bronze.

It would indeed be difficult to find anyone to equal them. The only Olympian remaining in the Russian team was Nelli Kim. The Rumanians, their closest rivals, still had most of the team silver medallists from Montreal including the incredible Nadia Comaneci — the little girl who had now grown up. In a few hours we would be able to pass our own judgment on this remarkable young lady.

Unfortunately, when watching a gymnast of Comaneci's reputation it is inevitable that her present performance will be compared with her past achievements, and this was certainly

Right
The women of East Germany regularly fill many of the medal-winning positions at major world events and their enviable strength-in-depth is best typified by competitors like Kunhardt – seen here during her asymmetric bars routine. Kunhardt herself has never won a major title and yet is a consistently valuable member of her country's squad.

the case in Strasbourg. Now that she has grown up and matured, some of her former vivacity has been lost. Perhaps she might have retained her appeal and reputation if she had not tried to prolong her youthful image.

Her performance at Strasbourg, particularly on the floor, created confusion with audience and judges alike, and at the end of the day she and her team-mates were only a fraction behind the Russians, although many people felt that the gap should have been wider. Without doubt, the most exciting part of the day was to see the impeccable execution of the set exercises by the young Russian team. It could be said that there is only one way to interpret a set exercise, but by virtue of their perfect timing, poise and body extensions they performed it precisely, but with that indefinable quality that has hallmarked Russian girl gymnasts for so long.

The surprise team which earned so much of our attention was the U.S.A. girls. While their beam and floor sets were average, their vaulting and bar exercises were outstanding, and they were capable of adding that extra dimension to the bars set exercise whilst still remaining truthful to it. The British girls did not appear to work at their best and were rather disappointing as a team. Except for Susan Cheeseborough, who was outstanding, all were capable of giving far better performances.

At last, the day for voluntary exercises arrived and the audience already aroused by the events of the compulsory routines, crowded into the hall ready for an early start. For the next two days, we were to know the frustration of watching gymnastics at its best. Those who have seen for themselves a full World Championship programme will know what that means. In order that 150 gymnasts may perform and be judged on all six pieces of apparatus, all of it must be in use the whole time.

Left
One of the generation of "new" Russian women gymnasts, Natalia Shaposhnikova – seen here competing in floor exercises – first came to prominence during the 1977 World Cup where she won the vault gold medal and finished third overall. At Strasbourg in '78, she was again the overall bronze medallist. Note the modern trend of going bare-footed during the floor exercises.

Left
A traditionalist as regards her choice of footwear for the floor exercises, Russia's Elena Moukhina is perhaps the greatest all-round woman gymnast in the world at present. Winner of the combined gold medal at the 1978 World Championships, she also won golds on both the asymmetric bars and the beam at the 1977 European Championships and the 1977 World Cup, in addition to a gold shared with Maria Filatova in the floor exercises at the Europeans.

Below
Checking that her legs and feet are positioned with slide-rule accuracy, young Karola Sube of East Germany competes on the beam.

The gymnasts work in six groups of six and rotate around the arena from one piece of apparatus to another. This continues from 8.30 in the morning until 9.00 in the evening, for six days! Even as a spectator, this can be something of an ordeal and he or she could well, as a result, suffer from what has been named "gymdigestion" — trying to digest all that is seen.

The first day of the voluntary exercises was for men. The Cubans again showed a great deal of skill and enterprise on all six pieces of apparatus. Their vaults were again very impressive. They achieved scores ranging from 9.45 points to 9.7 points which they earned mostly by elevating themselves to great heights above the horse, and by hand spring front somersaults. As mentioned previously, they are men of great stature and strength, and this without doubt, must have been a distinct advantage to them. Their floor

exercises were even more impressive, and though on some occasions without perfect control, they nevertheless achieved a score of 47.85 points which put them into 4th place, and in front of the Japanese with a score of 47.7 points. Appropriately, the highest scoring Cuban was a fine and powerful man named Enrique Bravo.

After the Cuban contribution, the traditional battle between the Soviet Union and Japan began. The Russian team were three points down as the voluntary exercises competition began, and needed to use maximum skill and effort if they were to overtake their rivals. It was on the pommel horse that they unveiled an outstanding performance, given by Detiatin. On each piece of apparatus, the Russians were gradually pulling back the Japanese lead, but eventually, the task was to prove too much for them. At the last piece — the horizontal bar, the

deficit was down to .95 of a point; surely a reminder to the Russians and all gymnasts that it is the compulsory exercises that determine the success or failure of all gymnastic competitions. The battle for the remaining places was just as hard fought with outstanding performances by the United States, East Germany, West Germany, France, Hungary and Rumania.

The climb to the medal class by the United States has been long and eventful. Until now, the Americans, both men and women have performed brilliantly in the United States, but have failed to impress continental judges.

Above
Caught suspended in his high bar routine is the young Bulgarian Stoian Deltchev. For many years one of his country's leading international competitors, Deltchev finished a highly-creditable eighth in the 1978 World combined exercises.

Right
Unquestionably the greatest gymnast ever to be produced by Hungary and the finest exponent ever of the pommel horse apparatus is Zoltan Magyar. He won his first pommel horse gold at the 1974 World Championships and in succeeding Olympic, European and World Cup competitions he has reigned supreme. His score of 9.90 during the 1978 Strasbourg combined exercises was the best achieved by any competitor.

Many will remember Doris Brause's performance on the asymmetric bars at Dortmund in 1966 — one of the greatest bars routines of all time, yet one which did not qualify for the finals!

The breakthrough came for the Americans at Strasbourg, and was not only impressive, but conclusive. It was Bart Connor and Kurt Thomas who, in the men's team, made the greatest impact with overall positions of 11th and 12th. Brilliant performances were given by Connor on pommels, parallels and vault, and Kurt Thomas giving one of the greatest performances of the championships to win the gold medal for floor exercises.

Eberhard Gienger of West Germany is a gymnast of extraordinary capabilities. Four years ago, his position in World championships was 15th overall, and a gold medal on horizontal bar was the reward for his outstanding performance. On this occasion, his overall position rose to sixth and he earned silver medals on the bar and pommels, with only the great gymnast Zoltan Magyar of Hungary beating him on this latter piece of apparatus. Gienger's influence and inspiration has done much to lift the West German team from a position of mediocrity, to being one of the top gymnastic countries in the world.

Zoltan Magyar, the man who beat Gienger on pommels is another whose outstanding prowess, albeit on one piece of equipment only, has made him a legend in gymnastics. He and Ferenc Donath, also of Hungary, were responsible for helping their team to fourth place overall. This was just .6 of a point ahead of the United States team. Much lower down the team placings in 12th position came Bulgaria. They would have been placed lower, had it not been for the brilliant performance of their 19-year-old all rounder Stoian Deltchev. His contribution to these championships, and his part in the European Championships of 1977,

Left
Leading the challenge of the United States during the eighties is Kurt Thomas, the highest-placed American in the combined exercises at the 1978 World Championships where he finished in 6th place – less than half a mark from winning a bronze medal. Although Thomas scored well in this particular high bar routine, he was let down by poor performances on the rings and parallel bars.

mark him as an experienced young man with a great future.

The host country is usually credited with having the advantage. Certainly, strong support from a friendly audience and local press helps to boost morale. Taking this into consideration, on this occasion in Strasbourg, when the top three French gymnasts were performing on the rings, their scores did not appear to agree with their apparently high standards of performance. Henry Boerio gave a very good performance and received a score of 9.4 points. Michael Boutard gave a fine routine with a full twisting double back somié finish, and again the score was only 9.4 points. They were followed by the popular Willy Moy. In his exercise, he displayed a perfect crucifix position, to finish with a full twisting double back somié finish. When his score came up, it, too, was only 9.4 points. The audience erupted with shouts of disapproval. They maintained this for so long that the men's jury intervened, and the closed circuit television recordings were consulted and replayed many times. Eventually, his score was amended to 9.5 points.

The women's voluntary exercises had promised to be the highlight of the championships. In the excitement of Russia — Rumania confrontation, it would have been easy to overlook the equally exciting competition taking place at the same time, between East Germany, Hungary and the United States. For the first time, an English-speaking gymnastic team had reached a top position among the medal contenders, and here at last we were about to see eastern European competitors defeated.

In the competition between Russia and Rumania, I felt that the Russian gymnasts, Moukhina, Shaposhnikova and Kim were a fair match for the Rumanians, Comaneci, Eberle and Ungureanu. Comaneci is still the favourite of the crowds. At the age of 18, her vaulting skill is still superb and her tussle with Kim resulted in the best vaulting of the day. On the beam it was Shaposhnikova v. Comaneci with the Russian girl displaying a completely new range of skills and balances. The most outstanding feat of her performance was when she commenced with a hand stand, and went to front lever across the beam, with her body lowered to almost a horizontal position, and her legs in wide splits. I am sure that hereafter, that position will be known as a "Shaposhnikova" even though it might be difficult to pronounce. Her score for this was 9.9!

Comaneci then countered with her exercise, based upon her original routine, and was almost without fault. The audience loved it, and she, too, was awarded 9.9 points. It must tax the judges' skill to separate two performances as fine as they were; one composed almost entirely of new and exacting skills, whilst the other,

Above
The rise to prominence of Rumania does not owe all to Nadia Comaneci. Able to hold her own in even the most exalted company is Teodora Ungureanu, a silver medallist in the floor exercises at the 1975 World Cup and a medal-winner on many other occasions since.

Left
The rings apparatus, probably more than any other, requires not only agility and balance on the part of competitors, but sheer strength, too. Here the Russian Vladimir Tikhonov steadies himself before launching into a backwards full twisting dismount.

though more of a routine nature, was still equally as well executed. On the bars, Comaneci appeared to have difficulty in giving a performance up to her previous standards, when she could only reach 9.7 points. On this occasion, Moukhina gave a better performance and gave her incredible version of Korbut's back flip to catch the high bar, but also with an additional twist. It was an outstanding exercise which impressed the judges and audience alike, and her score of 9.9 points was well received, although some had expected a maximum score.

In the other tussle between the East German girls, the Hungarians and the United States, it was Marcia Frederick, the American girl, who stole the day. Her performance contained so much in it reminiscent of a man's horizontal bar exercise, that many male gymnasts in the hall were astounded by her achievements, which culminated in a high piked shoot front somié with a full twist. This was the identical routine we saw three days later in the apparatus finals, and earned Marcia Frederick a score of 9.95 points, the gold medal and the World title on asymmetric bars. The Americans had not yet finished, for as they moved round to the floor exercises, all eyes were turning to focus upon the elegant Kathy Johnson. Her style and range of movement had already captured the audience. Kathy's style was based on what a few years ago would be considered the contemporary classic style, combined with a modern pop routine.

There were three medal-winners on floor exercises; Moukhina and Kim shared gold, and Johnson took the bronze. Even though Moukhina and Kim performed brilliantly, I am sure Kathy Johnson's exercise will long be remembered for its classical combination of skill and beauty. The Americans again had success with a vault finalist named Rhonda Schwandt, and had it not been for a low score in her compulsory vault exercise, she would have attained sufficient marks to carry her into the medal class. Her compulsory vault scored 9.45 points, but her voluntary earned her a score of 9.9 points. She was placed fourth in the vault final and ninth in the overall championships. Kathy Johnson, the best all round gymnast in the United States team came eighth in the overall reckonings. The United States gave warning at Strasbourg that they now have several world class gymnasts and will probably start to feature regularly amongst the medals.

The British girls could not match the performances I have just described, even though Susan Cheeseborough gave her own best ever performance and reached a high nine-point average. Likewise, the performance of British champion Ian Neale was outstanding. His overall score of 111.40 points is an all-time maximum for any British gymnast in world-class competition. His average score was 9.28 points. Both Ian Neale and Susan Cheeseborough will have received the coveted gold F.I.G. insignia, which gives them recognition as gymnasts of world class.

Below
Russia's Elena Moukhina, overall World champion in 1978, competes in the beam exercises on her way to the title. Despite the seeming excellence of her poise and balance seen here, this particular routine brought Moukhina her lowest score of the tournament – a "mere" 9.85!

The Apparatus

Parallel bars, horizontal bar, rings, horse, beam and floor

At any major gymnastics event such as those we see at Wembley each year and the one at Strasbourg in 1978, the first and most impressive sight is the apparatus, neat and orderly, arranged on the podium. The podium came into being just over 20 years ago and was an immediate success. Hitherto, everything took place at floor level and the impedimenta of the competition — scoreboards, piano, TV cameras, judges, scorers and photographers — were all more prominent than the gymnast. It is, therefore, a vital but nonetheless expensive item in any major gymnastic event. At Wembley, the British Amateur Gymnastics Associated staff erect the podium — a job so complex that it takes 12 men up to 24 hours to erect, and about half as long to dismantle.

Left
Czechoslovakia's Jiri Tabak demonstrates a double leg circle with side travel on the pommel horse during the 1978 Champions All tournament in London. Although not particularly a pommel horse specialist Tabak nevertheless shows here the poise of a top-class international gymnast.

Horse
Pride of place must surely go to the horse. It is the oldest member of the gymnastic family. Many centuries ago, warriors on horseback depended upon their horse in a battle. But it was not enough to have a fine horse. To survive, the warrior had to be a good horseman, too, and so many hours would be spent in the saddle of a wooden dummy horse. Horsemen would practise correct riding posture, and would learn how to mount and dismount. One can well imagine the young dare-devil of the day devising other exercises and how he would soon be vaulting right over it.

This wooden horse and the games that were played on it were no doubt handed down through the ages until this dumb steed found its way into the *Hasenheid* gymnasium of Friedrich Jahn. We know that he did have one, in fact many at one time, and a strange "animal" it looks to our modern eyes, complete with a high raised neck, a long hairy tail and a cumbersome saddle with ungainly pommel handles. Jahn had no doubt heard of the tricks that could be performed on the horse and invented even more. He then simplified the pommel handles so that they could be more easily gripped, and

thereby make easier lifting the legs over the horse's tail.

At about the time Jahn was having ideas about the pommels, Pehr Ling in Sweden was contemplating something quite outrageous. Ling had also inherited a wooden horse, and he decided to take the pommels off completely! The reason for this was that Ling's interest in the horse was to vault over it, and the pommels just got in the way. Jahn wanted to perform exercises using the pommels, whilst Ling went even further and eliminated the horse completely and replaced it with a box padded at the top. It is not on record what Jahn said when he heard of this, but he might well have considered it to be sacrilege.

Left
Cheeks puffed out with effort and concentration, Japan's brilliant Eizo Kenmotsu competes in the vault during the 1978 World Championships, where he finished as the overall combined silver medallist behind the Russian Nikolai Andrianov. Although the vault is not particularly one of Kenmotsu's great strengths, he still scored 9.8 for this effort.

Above
Although "pairs" gymnastics are not – as yet – included in the Olympic programme, demonstrations like this one, performed on the pommel horse by two Chinese gymnasts in London, make spectacular and exciting viewing for spectators. The great art in this particular routine is the execution of double leg circles performed simultaneously – and without either man knocking the other off.

Right
Despite the occasional below-par performance Russia's Alexandre Tkachev is still one of that country's leading male gymnasts of the seventies, finishing with a combined exercises bronze in the 1977 World Cup. Here Tkachev achieves a typically soaring dismount during a vault.

Fortunately for posterity the two men continued to pursue their conflicting beliefs, with the result that we now have both a pommel horse and a vaulting horse.

In the U.S.A., the horse with pommels is called the side horse, in Britain it is called the pommel horse. It could be suggested that confusion would be avoided by calling the horse with pommels the "Jahn Horse" and the horse for vaulting the "Ling Horse". We would then all know what we mean, and it would be a fine way to perpetuate the memory of two of the great "fathers of gymnastics". The pommel horse, Jahn's horse, is used now by only men and boys, although during the years between the two wars, the "brazen hussies" were making a brave effort to master this strength-demanding apparatus. It demands very great muscular power in arms and shoulders.

The weight of the body is supported by them while the body swings pendulum-fashion from side to side and forward and back, as the horse is enclosed by the continual sweep of the legs. The hands have to work very hard as they grasp and regrasp the pommels, allowing the legs to pass beneath them, yet always providing the power to keep the pendulum swinging.

Ling's horse, the vaulting horse, is used by all gymnasts and, because it requires very little strength, is to be found either as horse or box in every club, school and college in the world. In competitive form it is used lengthways for boys and men and sideways for girls and women. In the learning stages however, and for beginners, the sideways approach is always advisable.

Right
An unusual head-on view of Rumania's Nadia Comaneci competing in the vault. Although below her own supremely high standards at Strasbourg – she could only finish fourth behind the Russian trio of Moukhina, Kim and Shaposhnikova this particular vault was performed during practice.

Left
A twisting vault – a perfect example – as performed by Nadia Comaneci. Timing, positioning and above all confidence are absolutely crucial in this particular vault.

Below
East Germany's Angelika Hellmann in the primary stages of a twisting vault. Note how the body demonstrates perfect style and control. Hellmann shared the vault gold with Russia's legendary Ludmila Tourischeva at the 1973 European Championships, both scoring a total of 18.85 points.

Left

Originally built with such supreme strength and rigidity that they were rumoured to be able to withstand the weight of an elephant, parallel bars used in modern competition are now relatively supple, blending with a gymnast's swinging movements in a sympathetic harmony designed to complement the fluidity of routines.

Below

The great Japanese gymnast Mitsuo Tsukahara at the top end of a support swing. Tsukahara – innovator of the vault that bears his name – has been a major force in world gymnastics throughout much of the seventies and for sheer consistency has few rivals in the world. He first came to prominence during the 1970 World Championships.

Parallel Bars

Parallel bars are next on the list, not because they are of great antiquity (they are, in fact, the most recent of men's equipment) but because they are related to Jahn's pommel horse. Jahn soon discovered that few of his men had the arm strength to perform even the most basic of the required exercises. He then devised a simple strength-training device — two bars the same width apart and a little higher than the pommel handles, supported on four wooden uprights. So, clutching the bars one in each hand, they would lift themselves up and down, pumping strength and power into arms and shoulders. How many times since have gymnasts suffered the self-imposed agony of those press-ups?

Soon the bars were to become favourite play items as their versatility was explored and skill, as opposed to brute strength, became the requisite of the parallel bars. Imagine the excitement that must have prevailed when a gymnast swung himself aloft, upside down in handstand support for the first time.

With the introduction of women to gymnastics, the initiation rites were no less painful, and they struggled bravely in a world considered by many to be foolhardy even for the stronger sex. The parallel bars and the horizontal bar, the origins of which we shall explore in due course, were the "frightening devices of the devil" according to some.

Rather than admit defeat, the

Above

A Diamidov pirret – one of the most impressive moments in any gymnast's routine on the parallel bars. As can be seen, it is a movement requiring both perfect balance and strength.

determined young ladies who had dared to enter this men's world sought a compromise. Why not combine them into a pair of high and low horizontal parallel bars? The conversion no doubt came slowly. No one could quite decide whether the new contraption was two horizontal bars or a top heavy, lop-sided pair of parallel bars. How should they be used? Should the technique be the one used for parallels or as for a horizontal? There were many problems to be solved.

Today, we only need to see a young schoolgirl gymnast performing on them to know that they got their answers right. We, the amazed onlookers, still may not know what to call the bars — high and low — asymmetric — unevens? However, the girls certainly discovered how to use them!

Horizontal Bar

The horizontal bar unlike its young brother, the parallel bars, has no known origins. Its origin has been lost in the depths of history, but surely it is the one piece of apparatus, albeit in crude form, to which we can all relate. We all remember the sensation and freedom of swinging on the branches of trees when young. This leaves no doubt that our ancestors were once very much at home there.

Above left
The American Bill Hartung in the act of finishing a wheel manoevre with a twist to handstand – a tricky routine only capable of being performed by top-grade gymnasts and therefore usually only seen in internationals.

Right
Lasok of Poland going through his high bar routine. In the eyes of many spectators, this particular piece of apparatus lends itself to some of the most graceful and rhythmic routines seen in international men's gymnastics.

Left
Britain's Ian Neale executing a straddle piked swing. Although Britain is by no means one of the world's leading gymnastic nations, Neale still finished in 34th position at the 1978 World Championships, earning 9.5 points here.

Below
The utter perfection of Nadia Comaneci on the asymmetric bars is now legendary and best typified by her extraordinary 10 point maximum for this routine at the Montreal Olympics. Her score was due in no small part to her version of the Radochla somersault, shown here.

The first records of men performing on a bar are of the wandering acrobats and circus performers of the Middle Ages, but more often the bar was a rope pulled tight between two trees. Our entertainers would then give a double show — tight rope walker and horizontal rope performer. It was inevitable that the *Hasenheid* was to attract many types of bars and that Jahn should show considerable interest in the development of them and to experiment with the type of exercises to be performed. It is, today, essentially a man's apparatus and, for senior competition, the bar is adjusted to about 8ft. This just permits sufficient clearance as the gymnast performs his grand circles or giant swings as they are variously called. For basic training, it is adjusted to the more convenient and safe height of 4ft. to 5ft., according to the size of gymnast. It is in this form that the bar is most valuable for boys and girls.

In the previous story of the parallel bars we saw how the girls succeeded in combining the skill of the parallel bars with that of the horizontal bar. They have achieved this by studying the technique of the bar exercises and learning them on the low horizontal bar. It is quite a common sight in any modern gymnasium to see young boys and girls learning identical basic skills on the low horizontal bar. In its high form the bar has become the most exciting and skill-packed of all gymnastic pieces. It well deserves its title, "King of the Apparatus".

Right

Russia's Ludmila Tourischeva, perhaps the greatest woman gymnast of all time, demonstrates a layout half turn on the asymmetric bars. In the 1973 European Championships, Tourischeva won every women's gold medal and additionally was overall women's champion at the '72 Olympics, '74 World Championships and '75 World Cup.

Below right

The irrepressible Olga Korbut in dazzling action. At the 1972 Olympics she won the silver medal on this particular apparatus, just 0.22 points behind the great East German Karen Janz – the asymmetric bars were considered to be amongst the strongest of their disciplines.

Rings

Whilst our horizontal-bar-cum-tight-rope-walker was entertaining the locals, his partners would be setting up his rings in a nearby tree in readiness for his show. Both are typical members of a troupe of wandering players and acrobats. They were popular during the Middle Ages and provided the only form of professional entertainment then available. Their expertise, which included clowning, singing, juggling and tumbling was mostly very crude with the emphasis on ribald comedy. It was important for these wandering entertainers that their gear be light and portable, hence the popularity of ropes and rings.

Apparatus similar to this was eventually to be found hanging from the trees or from large timber gantries in the outdoor *Hasenheid* gymnasium. It was obviously refined by Jahn and his gymnasts, who soon developed two distinct patterns of skills upon them — the swinging rings and the still rings. The swinging rings became the popular play activity for the young boys and eventually the girls. The still rings became the prerogative of the strong man. Swinging rings, or flying rings as the Americans call them, were still used competitively in the U.S.A. until a few years ago.

A modern ring routine would be confined to still exercises, but here an explanation is needed.

Above right
Another brilliant Russian Alexandre Detiatin demonstrates the planche – one of the hardest of all positions on the rings. Detiatin won the Olympic silver medal on the rings at Montreal.

Right
The first American man to seriously challenge the Russian-Japanese monopoly in the post-war era was Peter Kormann, winner of a bronze in the floor exercises in Montreal. Here, he's on the rings.

Left
Demonstrating an L-support is world champion Nikolai Andrianov of Russia, one of the greatest gymnasts ever to emerge from that country. In addition to a combined gold in 1978, he was also the combined winner in the 1977 World Cup, the 1976 Olympics, the 1975 World Cup and the 1975 European Championships. He also won numerous individual gold, silver and bronze.

Below
Sheer delight shows on the face of Olga Korbut as she goes through one of her extra-special routines on the beam. Winner of this particular event at the Munich Olympics, Olga brought a new dimension to this particular piece of apparatus with technical skill allied to what, at times, seemed almost suicidal daring.

An exercise, if it is to satisfy F.I.G. rules, must have its correct proportion of swing, strength and held positions. Swing in that context means swinging of the body — not swinging of the rings. A rings exercise as we saw well illustrated in the World Championships, no longer belongs to the strong man, or "iron men" as they were once called, but instead to a man with a perfectly balanced physique. His exercise would be predominantly of perfectly controlled swinging skills, with a smaller proportion of held positions and of strength movements.

Balance Beam
The balance beam, like the asymmetric bars, was introduced as a means of stifling the criticism that women and girls were unsuited to perform on men's apparatus. Both were intended to develop a style of gymnastics more in keeping with the physical limitations of the female body and also to reduce risk and to limit the use of strength. With that in mind, it appears ludicrous now when viewing a modern girl performing on beam or bars.

Things have not turned out quite as intended, yet we cannot help feeling

grateful to the critics whose concern inspired the introduction of those two pieces of essentially feminine apparatus. The beam especially is the girls' piece. It bears no resemblance to any of the men's apparatus, nor has it been developed from any man's activity. It was first used early in the present century, but until the influence of the Russians since 1952, it was used purely as a beam for balancing, with no risk and very little skill was shown. It is now used to perform nearly every tumbling skill which is executed upon the floor, and yet still retains its original purpose of showing the performer balanced high upon her slim pedestal, in all her feminine charm and elegance.

The Floor

The floor exercise as we know it today is the youngest of all the gymnastic disciplines. The first men's Olympic Games floor exercise was included in the 1932 Olympiad. It was introduced to the women's programme in 1952. Hitherto, all floor exercises had taken the form of a team event with up to 60 performing together. For example, these were the "ground rules" for the Olympic Games of 1908. They were headed: *"Floor team competition. Voluntary Men's Exercises.*

"The exercises may be those known as free exercises, or exercises with hand apparatus or any combination of both or either. Teams of not less than 16 or more than 40. Time limit; 30 minutes".

Such events might well seem tame by today's standards, but one does remember one outstanding exception.

Far left
The new "baby" of the Russian side is Natalia Shaposhnikova, who came third overall at the 1978 World Championships. This particular floor exercise routine won her 9.8 points.

Above left
One of the few girls capable of challenging Russian domination in recent years has been Angelika Hellmann of East Germany, seen during a floor exercise.

Left
The current women's world champion Elena Moukhina in action in Strasbourg. This floor exercise gave her a near perfect score of 9.95 points.

The occasion was the Czech Spartakiade in Prague. Sixteen thousand gymnasts performed a mass exercise before an audience of 200,000 and such an exercise cannot be easily forgotten!

Today's women's floor exercise is a hybrid. Furthermore, it has no apparatus to tie it down to a set pattern or rhythm. It can easily adapt itself to the fashionable style of the day. Its mood can be classical or modern, jazz or pop or a mixture of these. The only essential requirement is that it must contain skill, not only in the tumbles, but also in its artistic expression.

The men's exercise, although without music, must also contain, in addition to the tumbling skills, movements of artistic quality. Both male and female gymnast must never forget that voluntary exercises, especially the floor exercises are their creation and should show their mood and express their feelings. Women's exercises have for some years caused considerable controversy due to the difficulty in defining what is an artistic performance. It is obviously not easy to judge, and different judges have different views. The quality of tumbling skills can almost be catalogued and measured with computer-like accuracy, but assessing the quality of artistic expression is a much more elusive task as the beauty is more often than not in each judge's eye.

Above
Nikolai Andrianov on his way to a combined exercises gold and the current world championship crown. He also won the floor exercise gold at the 1977 World Cup, the '76 Olympics, the '75 Europeans, '73 Europeans and the '72 Olympics – remarkably consistent gymnastics.

Right
Although quite popular throughout the world as an adjunct to gymnastics, acrobatics is still regarded in some circles as belonging more to the circus ring than to serious international competition. Despite this rather narrow view, however, there are regular acrobatics championships throughout the world and the sport is particularly popular in the United States. Here, the Chinese Kuo Ching Tseng and Wei Hsing Pan demonstrate the strength and skill which are the hallmarks of really top-flight acrobatics.

The Innovators.

The select few
who create gymnastics

Throughout the history of any sport, and gymnastics is not an exception, there are always the exceptionally talented performers: those who bring the sport alive with their incredible and dramatic daring. In gymnastics these innovators are heroes and heroines. Their movements off the bars, beam, vault or floor — often high above the floor — require courage and artistry way beyond the levels held in normal routines. Without doubt, there are many men and women who perform equally difficult sequences, and programmes, in competition after competition; however, now and then an incredibly bright light is beamed onto the scene. The occasional breath-taking manoeuver is executed, the audiences, coaches and fellow competitors can only stand and admire. The move is then analysed, isolated, repeated and incorporated into the various Olympic, World or National Championship routines. In the pages that follow we have selected a few of these outstanding athletes.

Left
More than anyone else, Olga Korbut, with her performances at the 1972 Munich Olympics, helped turn gymnastics into one of the most popular sports in the world today. One of her great fortés was mesmerising routines like this on the asymmetric bars.

Korbut

Olga Korbut is a Soviet Union gymnast, and it was in Munich in 1972, that the world first saw the Korbut brand of gymnastics, which was to change the style of many young female performers. Her performance on the bars was unique, but the most memorable and frequently imitated part was the back flip from standing to catching the top bar.

Also at the Munich Olympics, and equally outstanding, Olga introduced, on the beam, a standing back somersault. Since then we have seen Olga Korbut, and others, perform the "Korbut back flip" on bars many times, and it is even embellished now with a complete full twist between leaving the top bar and re-catching it. Olga Korbut is now married and retired from gymnastics but has given so much to the sport. Her high, hollow-back somersault to chest roll was a spectacular part of her floor routine, although it is seldom attempted now even in today's competitions.

Radochla

Brigit Radochla was one of East Germany's good all-round gymnasts of the early Sixties, but was never in the gold-medal class. Her claim to fame was the puzzling somersault move which she put into her asymmetric bars routine at the European Championships, in Sofia, in 1965. Like Diamidov's turn, or pirouette as it was sometimes called, its speed of execution deceived the eyes. It was, in fact, a forward somersault from a "hands in front" position, with support from the low bar to catch the top bar, with the legs wide in side-straddle position.

Since then, there have been many variations. They are now performed safely by many young girls, but it can be a dangerous exercise when performing initially, unless there is the added protection of soft mats.

Comaneci

Nadia Comaneci of Rumania is, like Olga Korbut, renowned not for any one isolated skill, but for bringing a complete new image to gymnastics, supported by a range of skills hitherto unknown.

However, the majority of the young gymnasts throughout the world place the highest esteem on her somersault between the asymmetric bars.

The "Comaneci somersault" is closely related to the Radochla routine, with the difference being that the Comaneci starts from a backward swing on the high bar through a very high forward straddle somersault to re-grasp the high bar. Comaneci achieves incredible height above the bar before re-catching it, from an unsighted position, as clearly illustrated by her on the opposite page.

Above

Giving a prime example of a Radochla somersault on the asymmetric bars is the Russian Arzhanikova.

Right

Nadia Comaneci of Rumania superseded Olga Korbut in the eyes of the public with a series of tremendous displays at the 1976 Montreal Olympics. Her gold medal in the asymmetric bars was won with a hitherto-unachieved perfect 20 points.

Above

One of the first Russians to establish themselves in international competition was Albert Azarian, here demonstrating the "iron cross".

Azarian

Albert Azarian of the Soviet Union was one of the world's greatest gymnasts. His favourite apparatus was the rings, and he was often known as "king of the rings". On this apparatus he won the gold medal at the 1956 Olympics and again at the 1960 Olympics. He was also gold medallist at the 1954 and 1958 World Championships on this testing apparatus.

Known as "the iron man" he is best remembered for his Olympic crucifix, or the "Azarian iron cross", as it is now referred to. He was one of the last of the generation of strong men and his iron cross is seldom seen now because skills demanding such terrific strength are no longer encouraged. However, a beautiful replica of Azarian's iron cross was performed at the 1978 Strasbourg World Championships by the youngest member of the Soviet team. This member was Edward Azarian — son of Albert. A proud moment surely for Albert Azarian and his wife, who were both in Strasbourg as official coaches to the young and talented Dutch team.

Stalder

Josef Stalder of Switzerland was one of the great gymnasts of the years immediately following World War Two. In the Olympic Games in London, 1948, he became champion on the horizontal bar and was awarded the silver medal for the same event in 1952 at Helsinki. It is for horizontal bar work that Stalder's name will always be remembered. He performed for the first time a clear circle on the bar from hand-stand to hand-stand, passing through straddle support. It is now performed by men and women with numerous variations.

Above

Following in his father's footsteps and perhaps destined to be a Russian star of the eighties is Edward Azarian, seen with his own version of his father's iron cross, at the 1978 World Championships.

Diamidov

Serguei Diamidov of the Soviet
Union was overshadowed by the
unknown boy Voronin at Dortmund in
1966, but his claim to gymnastic
immortality was nevertheless
assured. During those World Championships, he performed a parallel bar
exercise which, besides earning him a
gold medal, amazed the gymnastic
world. In the middle of his routine, he
appeared to complete a 360-degree
turn in handstand position, whilst
keeping one hand on the equipment.
This invited the comment that if he
were to perform this movement twice
in succession his arm would drop off.

At first, no one knew how it was done
or how to describe it, so it just became
known as a "Diamidov". Even today, it
is still a difficult movement to perform
for most of the world's top gymnasts.

Menichelli

Italy's Franco Menichelli has
influenced the style of the men's floor
exercise more than any other gymnast.
The floor exercise as we now know it
had broken away from the team exercise format three decades earlier and it
seemed as though the gymnastic leaders of the day were not sure which way
to go. During the Olympics of 1964 this
slightly-built young Italian seemed to
show the world the way.

Until this time, men gymnasts had
tried to enhance their floor exercise
performances by their immaculate
dress. However Menichelli had no such
pretensions. What he was going to
perform needed no enhancing and he
took the floor in what was described at
the time as the "Peter Pan look": the
blue Italian national vest, white
shorts, socks and gym slippers.

The performance he gave then and
repeated many times during the following eight years was the most
advanced exercise of tumbling ever
seen. Without sacrificing any gymnastic qualities he sprung, soared, flipped
and somersaulted from one corner to
another. The spellbound audience held
its breath as he produced almost 90
seconds of gymnastic genius, and one
part of the exercise was even more
vividly memorable than the rest. This
was when he ran two or three cat-like
steps, half turned into an "arabian"
then rose off the floor higher and
higher, turning gracefully in the air
before plunging back to the floor with a
forward roll. A truly magical moment,
since which that Arabian high dive
forward roll has been attempted by
gymnasts all over the world, but never
quite with the Menichelli skill.

Cerar

Miroslav Cerar of Yugoslavia will always be remembered as the gymnast who rejuvenated the pommel horse. A typical horse exercise of his period — he took the gold at the 1968 Olympics — was based upon the time-honoured leg circles, scissors and an occasional travel along the length of the horse to show virtuosity, the legs continually moving, swinging and circling, but always pointing downwards. Except to the purist, there was a danger of the exercise becoming monotonous, and the audience was never expected to gasp with delight — only sigh with relief when the exercise was completed without mishap.

Cerar may have resented this since the horse was, after all, the oldest and most revered friend of gymnasts, and it deserved a more exciting exercise. So he, too, circled the horse and scissored, and travelled along it, then came back to the pommels and raised his superbly straight legs aloft. For a fraction of time each leg in turn would be poised, pointing upwards, and the audience —

including the purists — felt the delight and wonder Cerar had given to the gymnasts' dumb friend, the pommel horse.

Voronin

Mikhail Voronin was one of many Soviet Union gymnasts to make a lasting impression on enthusiasts throughout the world since his dramatic entry 15 years ago. He was overall World Champion at Dortmund in 1966 and won a silver medal in Mexico two years later. It was on the horizontal bar that he gave his name to the "Voronin hop". It is a high-piked front vault over the bar to re-grasp the other side. This is an exciting skill when performed with Voronin's height and smooth control, and is now used extensively by women as well as men gymnasts at the top level.

Above left
Between 1968 and 1970, Miroslav Cerar was unbeatable on the pommel horse. Olympic, World and European champion during that period, his trademark was unrivalled technical perfection.

Above
Mikhail Voronin demonstrates the "hop" over the high bar to which the great Russian athlete gave his name.

Yamashita

The vault of Japanese gymnast Haruhiro Yamashita, unleashed at the Prague World Championships in 1962, which later won him the event gold medal at the Olympic Games two years later, became the most renowned gymnastic skill for almost a decade. Many gymnasts found the vault itself easy to copy, but great arm and shoulder power, together with split second body control, are required if the correct height and body shape is to be achieved. Many young boys and girls now include the Yamashita in their repertoire.

Tsukahara

Mitsuo Tsukahara was the Japanese team-mate of Yamashita who gave his name to the backward somersault off the hands, first seen at the 1970 World Championships. Again, this vault is extremely difficult to perform in the true style, requiring a great thrust from the arms and shoulders, followed by a half turn on to the horse, together with a tight tuck of the body in order to turn one and a half times, landing on the feet.

Many variations of the Tsukahara have since been introduced adding great complexity and risk to the performance. These include the piked back somersault, the straight-backed somersault and somersaults including half and full twists.

Above left
Franco Menichelli, Italian star of the Sixties, shows the control required to pull off the Yamashita vault.

Above right
Mitsuo Tsukahara during his backward somersault off the horse which made the Japanese athlete one of the great innovators of the sport. This exercise demonstrates his Tsukahara vault in straight position.

The Major Countries

Soviet Union, East Germany, Rumania, West Germany, Japan and USA

Russia

It was Sunday, August 27, 1972; the venue: the Olympic *Sporthalle* in Munich. It was the first day of a Games that were later to become remembered for tragic events away from the competitive arena, but the minds of the spectators in the *Sporthalle* were still untroubled by the terrible hours that were to come. They were enjoying the opening exercises in the gymnastics competition, marvelling at the expertise of some of the finest gymnasts in the world. As expected, the men of Japan, Russia and East Germany reigned supreme, while the women's events, in common with each previous Olympic tournament since 1952, were dominated by the Russians.

One competitor in particular, however, caught both the public's eye and imagination. A tiny, waif-like figure under 5ft. in height and appearing far younger than her actual 17 years

performed with such charm and style — allied to superb technical accomplishment — that she totally captivated a world-wide television audience and practically single-handed turned gymnastics from being a minority-interest sport into the hugely popular, mass-appeal phenomenon which has engulfed the sport in just one decade.

The girl in question was, of course, Olga Korbut — perhaps the epitome of the Russian domination of world gymnastics that stretches back nearly 30 years. For although Japan's men have had the edge over their Russian counterparts in the Olympic and World competition in which they've met, the excellence of the Russian women — which no other nation has ever been able to seriously challenge — gives the U.S.S.R. a virtually unshakeable supremacy over the rest of the world.

The Olympics of 1948 and the World Championships of 1950 were denied the benefit of Russian participation, but with the 1952 Olympics the position was to change dramatically. During those Games, the Russians took gold and silver in the men's combined exercises, plus silver in the parallel bars and gold in the vault, made a clean 1-2-3 sweep of the pommel horse, were first, second and equal third in the

Left
Caught in a typically classical pose, Olga Korbut at times seemed to defy gravity as she competed in the beam. Her slight figure, giving scant sign of outward strength, was still capable of gymnastic feats of great power.

rings and walked away with the team gold. The Russian women fared no less well: gold and silver in the combined exercises, silver on the bars and floor exercises, plus gold and silver on the beam and all three medals in the vault. And the team gold for good measure.

In the six Olympics between Helsinki and Montreal, the Russians have won one team gold and five silvers in the men's events and six golds in the women's, while in seven World Championships between 1954 and 1978, Russia's team medal tally is two golds and five silvers for the men and six golds and a silver for the women.

Add to that countless individual medals and you begin to get an idea not only of Russia's domination, but also of her consistency in being able to produce both male and female competitors of the highest international calibre.

Although it was Olga Korbut who captured hearts and imaginations in Munich, she was just one member of a Russian women's squad that included the outstanding athlete Ludmila Tourischeva who, despite performing in Korbut's shadow during the individual events, nevertheless won the combined exercises gold — a feat she also matched at the 1970 and 1974

Below
Poise and perfection from Ludmila Tourischeva, whose classical technical ability was the supreme counterpoint to Korbut's pyrotechnics. Her finest hours came when she won every single event in the 1973 European Championships – a feat she then repeated during the World Cup event, two years later.

Above

A pose that sums up to perfection the charm of Olga Korbut. Although it is easy to lose sight of the fact that she never during her sparkling career won a major overall title, she had the ability, especially on the beam and in the floor exercises, to completely captivate her audience.

World Championships. Perhaps her finest achievements, though, were winning every single gold medal in the 1973 European Championships (one shared), and all five — a record — in the 1975 World Cup. Many were expecting a similar clean sweep in Montreal the following year, but by then, a new Russian star had emerged.

While little Olga Korbut was the darling of the crowd in Munich, the Montreal favourite was the Rumanian Nadia Comaneci, but close behind her both competitively and in the popularity stakes was Nelli Kim who won two individual and one team gold plus a silver. In her two individual gold medal performances — the vault and the floor exercises — she matched Comaneci's scoring elsewhere by gaining two perfect 10s. In the 1978 World Championships, she was a member of the Russian gold medal-winning team and lost the overall title to her compatriot Moukhina by just 0.15 of a point.

In addition to Korbut and Kim, Russia has three other girls who seem destined to keep their country firmly in gold medal position in events yet to come. With Korbut and Tourischeva now retired, the mantle now rests upon Nelli Kim, Maria Filatova — the 1977 World Cup overall champion — Natalia Shaposhnikova, the vault gold

medallist at the same Championships and, of course, Elena Moukhina who in addition to her overall World title in 1978 also took the gold in the beam and the bars in the '77 World Cup. As if to underline Russian supremacy, the silver and bronze overall positions in 1978 were filled by Kim and Shaposhnikova and all indications are that this status quo will remain unaltered for some considerable time to come.

While the Russian women regularly sweep the board at international level, their male gymnasts — even in the face of tremendous opposition from Japan who have taken the team title at the last five Olympics and the last five World Championships — have acquitted themselves brilliantly, too, and none more so than Nikolai Andrianov, winner of the combined gold in the 1978 World Championships, the 1977 World Cup, the 1976 Olympics and the 1975 World Cup. Additionally, Andrianov has won over a dozen individual golds, silvers and bronzes while competing in these events.

One who could be Andrianov's successor is Vladimir Markelov, winner of the individual title at the 1977

Left
Alexandre Detiatin of Russia shows skill and perfection during his routine on the rings at the 1978 World Championships. Detiatin scored 9.7 for the routine and went on to finish in overall bronze medal position. One of the new generation of Russian male gymnasts, Detiatin is one who will be out to challenge Japanese supremacy in the 1980 Moscow Olympics and beyond.

World Student Games, who sprang to greater prominence by taking the individual gold at the 1977 European Championships in addition to tying for the combined gold with Andrianov during the World Cup that same year. Markelov also finished in gold medal position in the rings in the '77 European Championships and in the pommel horse and the vault during the World Cup, that same year. Two other young Russians to watch in the future are Alexandre Detiatin — third in the world in 1978 — and Alexandre Tkachev, who finished third behind Andrianov and Markelov in the overall 1977 World Cup standings, yet surprisingly could only come 11th overall in 1978 — surely a temporary lapse, for with a floor gold in the 1977 European event, he is clearly a gymnast of the highest calibre.

So the Russian gymnastic juggernaut rolls relentlessly on. With more than 3,000 gymnasia and hundreds of thousands competing in events from local to international standard, the country is geared to producing gold medal-winning performers not only for the 1980 Moscow Olympics, but way beyond.

Above left
Despite this mishap when the equipment collapsed during the 1975 World Cup competition, Ludmila Tourischeva won every single event – a suitable feat to commemorate the inauguration of this particular international contest.

Left
Determination shows on Olga Korbut's face as she competes in the beam – one of her great speciality events. Note the seemingly effortless combination of technical ability, poise and originality – all Korbut trademarks during her career.

Olympics at Munich, he took a gold in
the high bar and a bronze in the rings,
following this up with two golds — in
the high bar and rings — and a joint
silver in the parallel bars during the
1975 World Cup. At the '76 Olympics,
at the age of 28, this extraordinary
gymnast was once again in the medals
— gold in the bar, silver in the vault
and bronze in the parallel bars and
combined exercises. As awe-inspiring
as Tsukahara's achievements have
been, even they must take second place
to the man who is rightly judged to be
the finest all-round gymnast that
Japan has ever produced — Sawao
Kato. In 1968 in Mexico and 1972, in
Munich, Kato became only the third
man in history to win the combined
exercises gold twice and was only
denied a hat-trick of firsts by Russia's
mighty Nikolai Andrianov who took
the individual title in Montreal with a
total of 116.65 marks to Kato's
silver-medal performance of 115.65
points.

Kato headed the illustrious
Japanese trio of himself, Kenmotsu
and Nakayama who came first, second
and third respectively for the individual title at the '72 Olympics and he
also won an individual gold in the
parallel bars together with silvers in
the high bar and pommel horse — in
the latter event being just 0.125 of a
mark behind the Russian Klimenko.

Previously, in addition to his individual combined exercises gold at
Mexico in 1968, he led the way in
another Japanese 1-2-3 — this time in
the floor exercises at those Games —
and gained some consolation for his
combined silver at Montreal by taking
the gold four years later on the Munich
parallel bars. Indefatigably, he was
still competing in 1977 — nine years
after his first major triumph and at the
age of 31 — and was Japan's only
medal winner (with a bronze in the
parallel bars) during that year's World
Cup competition in which the only
non-Russian medal winners were

Japan

While acknowledging Russia's
claim to be the best overall gymnastics
nation in the world, there can be little
argument that when it comes to the
men alone, one country — Japan —
reigns supreme. In every major
championship between the 1960
Olympics and the 1978 World championships, the Japanese have won the
men's team event and although it is
open to discussion as to whether or not
the *individual* achievements of the
Russians outweigh those of the
Japanese, for sheer consistency the
latter cannot be faulted.

At Strasbourg in 1978, they pipped
Russia for the team gold by just 0.9 of a
mark with Eizo Kenmotsu, Hiroshi
Kajiyama and Shigeru Kasamatsu all
turning in brilliant performances and
it is competitors like these who will be
carrying Japan's future hopes.

Perhaps two of the greatest
Japanese gymnasts of all time are
Mitsuo Tsukahara and Haruhiro
Yamashita, both of whom have given
their names to vaults which they first
performed. Yamashita won the vault
gold appropriately enough at the
Tokyo Olympics in 1964, while
Tsukahara first came to the public eye
during the 1970 World Championships where he won a silver in the
combined exercises and the rings and
the gold in the vault. In the 1972

Gienger, who shared the high bar gold, Kato, who got the parallel bars bronze and Nikolai (East Germany) who shared the pommel gold. It was, perhaps, the only time since the 1960 Olympics that Japan's male gymnasts have been virtually eclipsed by their great Russian rivals.

While the men of Japan are all-supreme, the same cannot be said of their women gymnasts. Entering Olympic competition for the first time at Melbourne in 1956 they finished in sixth place, but they scooped a team bronze in the 1962 World Championships and repeated this performance on home ground during the 1964 Tokyo Olympics. They won the team bronze yet again at the 1966 World Championships, but that was destined to be their last team medal for at least 12 years as in intervening Olympic and World Championships they have finished out of the medal positions. At the most recent World Championships — at Strasbourg in 1978 — they could only finish 7th out of the 22 competing countries, some 18 points behind the gold medal-winning Russians, while in the individual classification, the Japanese trio of Yayoi Kano, Sakiko Nozawa and Yoshito Matsumoto ended up in 23rd, 24th and 28th places.

In past championships, however, notably during their team medal success period, Japanese women — while never even remotely challenging the superiority of the Russians — have acquitted themselves well. During the 1958 World Championships, Tonaka became Japan's first-ever woman medallist at top level with bronze medals in the beam and floor exercises and this was followed with a bronze for Ikeda on the beam — tying with Ducza of Hungary — during the 1962 World Championships. During the next World Championships in 1966, Ikeda had improved sufficiently to win the overall individual bronze together with a silver in the bars, but that proved to be Japan's last individual medal at top level up to the end of 1978.

Despite the strenuous efforts being made in Japan to improve the world standing of their women gymnasts, it is perhaps unlikely that sufficient improvement will be made in time for the 1980 Moscow Olympics, or even the 1982 World Championships in the United States. If anyone is to challenge the might of the Russians, Rumanians and East Germans in that time period, it is more likely to be the Americans than anyone else.

For the men of Japan, however,

these next two great gymnastic occasions give every indication of bringing a renewal of the sporting rivalry that exists between themselves and the Soviet Union. Their severest test will come when they meet the Russians on the latter's home territory in 1980, for this advantage could be just enough for the Russians to bridge the tiny points gap that invariably separates the gold and silver team and overall individual medal winners.

The 1977 World Cup, with just Kato's solo bronze standing between them and total anonymity, was a severe blow to Japan's pride and although they recovered to take the team gold at the World Champion-

Above
Shigeru Kasamatsu, seventh overall in 1978, during his pommel horse routine, for which he gained only 8.90 – a mark that prevented him from challenging for the medal positions. Owing to the supremacy of Hungary's Magyar, Japan has had few recent successes in this event.

ships a year later, the Russians still managed to win the overall individual gold and bronze with Kenmotsu's silver sandwiched between them.

Whatever is in store between these two great nations in 1980 and 1982, one thing is guaranteed — perhaps the greatest display of male gymnastics ever seen.

East Germany

If Russia can claim to be the best overall gymnastics nation in the world, running them a close second for that distinction would be East Germany, who for sheer consistency in championship after championship can match the Russians, but lack that infinitesimal edge in performance that separates gold medal winners from silver and bronze runners-up.

The East German women began to make their mark in the European Championships of 1959 in which Fost took the bronze in the asymmetric bars and vault. At the next European event two years later, Fost was joint third overall and picked up three more individual medals: silver in the vault and bronze in the beam and bars. In the 1964 Tokyo Olympics, it was the turn of the men. Although not winning a single individual medal, they were still consistent enough to pick up a team bronze behind Japan and Russia — a 1-2-3 placing that was destined to become extremely familiar over the next decade and beyond. Medals began to come thick and fast during the 1965

European Championships and in the 1966 World Championships the East German men repeated their feat of 1964 — not a single individual medal, yet a team bronze behind Japan and Russia. That story repeated itself in the men's event in the Mexico Olympic Games in 1968 and it was in that event that the East German women really asserted themselves, too, with the brilliant Karen Janz gaining a silver in the bars and helping her team to an overall bronze, helped by Zuchold's silver in the vault. In 1969, Janz became the overall European women's champion winning the gold in the bars, beam and vault and finishing just 0.05 of a mark behind the Russian Karassova to take a silver in the floor exercises. In the 1970 World Championships, the final team order in the men's events ran true to expectation with the usual trio of countries finishing in what must have seemed to the rest of the world as their by now allotted positions. However on this occasion East Germany actually won an individual medal through Koste, who finished equal with Hayata of

Japan for the bronze medal in the high bar. In the women's events, with Janz gaining a gold on the bars and a silver in the vault, Zuchold winning a combined silver plus gold in the beam and vault and Schmitt taking a bronze in the beam, East Germany finished second behind Russia in the team event.

At Munich in 1972, in addition to the usual men's team bronze award, Koste took gold in the vault, while in the women's events, Janz, despite competition from the likes of Korbut and Tourischeva, finished second overall and won gold in the bars and vault together with a bronze on the beam to consolidate their team silver.

In the inaugural World Cup competition in 1975, East Germany surprisingly failed to enter a team in either men's or women's events and at the 1976 Olympics the emergence of Rumania pushed the East German girls down into team bronze position.

Below
East Germany's Angelika Hellmann, for so long a rival to the greatest Russians, on the asymmetric bars.

The 1977 European Championships saw a new East German star rise to prominence — Ralph Barthel who shared both gold in the vault and silver in the parallel bars.

At Strasbourg in 1978, the same old song was played again, with a Japan-Russia-East Germany finish in the men's team event and a Russia-Rumania-East Germany line-up in the women's. In the individual overall classification, the men's bronze was shared by Michael Nikolay, Roland Bruckner and Barthel, who finished in 10th, 13th and 14th places respectively, while the women's bronze came with 7th, 11th and 15th placings for, respectively, Steffi Kraker, Silvia Hindorff and Birgit Suss. Although the East German men perhaps have come to expect their team bronze almost by divine right, the performance of the Americans at Strasbourg must have caused some anxiety. A mere 0.9 of a mark separated Japan and Russia, but East Germany, who finished over seven clear points behind Russia, must have had the occasional worried glance at the Americans who finished three points adrift of them. If that American improvement continues, the East Germans just possibly could find themselves both surprised and medal-less in Moscow. In the women's team event, however, the East Germans look to have a reasonably strong grip on their "traditional" bronze. A fairly hefty 4.5 marks separated Russia and Rumania at the top with East Germany — on 382.25 — exactly two points behind the latter. Fourth-placed Hungary were 4.65 points behind East Germany and the fifth — placed U.S.A. 5.05 points behind East Germany, and it might take until 1982 before that gap is narrowed and closed — if indeed it is, for although Karen Janz has long retired, Kraker, — she was second overall in the 1977 World Cup in addition to winning a silver on the beam and bronze in the bar and floor exercises — Hindorff and Suss are formidable competitors. So are Grabolle, Trantov and Kunhardt who all regularly appear in the national women's squad.

As far as the East German men are concerned, they suffered the embarrassment of seeing Wolfgang Thune, a European bronze medallist on the bar in 1973 and a World Championship silver medallist in the same event in 1974, defect to West Germany — for whom he now appears — but they still have Bruckner, Barthel, Nikolay, Mack and Jensch with whom to fight

Above and right
East German Silvia Hindorff, 11th overall in 1978, during her beam routine. Note the great elevation achieved – worth 9.7 from the judges.

off the inevitable American challenge over the next few years.

With the intensive training system used throughout the Eastern European bloc continuing to turn out a stream of international-class competitors, East Germany does have an advantage over the no less fiercely competitive, but somehow more relaxed, attitude of the United States. Years of finishing behind Japan and Russia in the men's events and behind Russia — and latterly Rumania — in the women's could however be starting to have a demoralising effect on the East Germans. They know that despite the occasional brilliant individual medal-winning performance, they can never really hope to overtake their traditional rivals and are therefore faced with the unenviable realisation that their place is there for the taking and that some countries are beginning to get uncomfortably close. Whether this acts as a spur or not will be seen in Moscow in 1980.

West Germany

For many years now, West Germany has been the top Western European gymnastics nation. Although they have never won a major team title, they have the happy knack of producing fine individual competitors who are regularly in the medal-winning positions at Olympic, World and European championships. Beginning with a bronze in the floor exercises through Schmitt in the 1957 European Championships to get their men off the medal mark, West Germany then took a combined bronze and a pommel horse bronze with Furst in the next Europeans and a silver in the same event in the subsequent Europeans.

After a lull during the remainder of the Sixties and into the early Seventies, West Germany re-emerged on the international scene with a gold medal for Eberhard Gienger on the bar during the 1973 European Championships, an event which also saw the country's first-ever major women's medallist — Utta Schorn who obtained a bronze in the vault. In 1974, Gienger repeated his gold on the bar with a brilliant 19.5 during the World Championships and in the 1975 European Championships he gained the distinction of finishing overall second behind Nikolai Andrianov, in addition to winning his third gold on the bar and a bronze in the pommel horse. In the

Above
A leading West German gymnast during his exercise routine on the floor.

first World Cup competition, also in 1975, Gienger found himself pushed off the bar top-spot by no less a competitor than Japan's Mitsuo Tsukahara who took the gold with 19.45 compared to Gienger's silver medal-winning 19.35. In the 1976 Montreal Olympics, Tsukahara again took the bar gold with a breathtaking 19.675 and his compatriot Kenmotsu won the silver, with Gienger, although scoring 19.475, down in third place. Gienger's astonishing run continued with a shared silver on the parallel bars in the 1977 European Championships, but the World Cup of that same year saw him right back to the peak of his ability on the high bar, scoring 19.6 to share the gold medal with the Russians Markelov and Tkachev. In 1978 at Strasbourg, this remarkable athlete finished fourth in the overall classification just 0.175 of a mark behind the bronze medal-winner Alexander Detiatin. To retain this sort of consistency over five years of international competition, marks Gienger as one of the outstanding gymnasts of the Seventies.

Despite finishing in overall fifth place at Strasbourg, the performance of the West German men's team was a shade disappointing. Although Gienger's contribution cannot be faulted, his compatriots Volker Rohrwick and Edgar Jorek could only end up in 17th and 27th places respectively, but with Thune now available for future competitions following his defection from East Germany in 1975, the West Germans must be reasonably optimistic about their prospects for one or two individual medals in 1980 and 1982. As far as the West German women are concerned, the prime consideration is improving on their single, solitary bronze won back in 1973. In common with the West German men, they were top Western European nation at Strasbourg, but even so could only come ninth behind Russia, Rumania, East Germany, Hungary, the U.S.A., Czechoslovakia, Japan and Canada, even though just 1.35 marks separated them from Japan.

As can be gained from this placing, the West German girls were well down in the overall classification with Annette Michler in 21st position and Petra Kurbjuweit and Annette Toifl 24th and 26th respectively. Coincidentally, all three girls scored their best marks — 9.65 — on the asymmetric bars, but their points for the other three disciplines were some way short of top international standards. In young Andrea Bieger, West Germany could have a gymnast to rival some of those from Eastern Europe, but the signs are that any future successes will come from the men.

Clearly Gienger cannot be expected to go on forever and much will depend on whether Thune can successfully adapt to the East-West transition. Of the other men, Rohrwick was below his own high standards in 1978 and can certainly improve on his overall 17th place. The West Germans have virtually no hope of realistically challenging Russian or Japanese supremacy in the men's events in the forseeable future, but it could be that a fascinating battle for the bronze between them, East Germany and the U.S.A. will take place in Moscow. That apart, it is to Gienger's successors that they must look for individual honours.

Below
In finishing fourth at the 1978 World Championships, West Germany's Eberhard Gienger achieved the highest placing of any Western gymnast.

Rumania

One of the most remarkable phenomena in the entire sporting spectrum — let alone the world of gymnastics — to have taken place during the Seventies has been the rise to prominence of Rumania in the field of women's gymnastics. Until 1976, when Nadia Comaneci and company dazzled the Montreal spectators with a display that exceeded the brilliance of Munich four years previously, Rumania were really very small fish in the pond of world gymnastics. Although her men had been singularly unsuccessful in capturing major international honours, her women had acquitted themselves with fair distinction at top level, regularly winning medals in European championships

Below
Another of the new breed of Rumanian girl gymnasts, Emilia Eberle was fifth overall at Strasbourg, but achieved a bronze medal on the beam.

and winning the team bronze at the 1956 and 1960 Olympics and also at the 1958 World Championships.

The 1973 European event gave a slight inkling of what was to come. Rumania took three individual bronze medals together with a silver, but all eyes were very much on the likes of Korbut and Tourischeva and quite understandably so, with the latter winning a gold medal in every event in the competition. In the 1974 World Championships, the only Rumanian name on the medal list was that of a man — Dan Grecu — who shared the gold in the rings with Nikolai Andrianov, but in the 1975 European Championships, Rumania's star shone with a new brightness. Grecu repeated his previous year's performance with a gold on the rings and his compatriot Mihail Bors finished 0.3 of a mark behind him for the silver. In the women's events however, Tourischeva and the new Russian prospect Nelli Kim were faced by a precocious 14-

year-old called Nadia Comaneci who not only won the individual combined gold, but came first in the bars, the beam and the vault, too, in addition to taking the silver behind Nelli Kim in the floor exercises. Although overshadowed by her countrywoman, Rumania's Goreac picked up a pair of bronze medals in the beam and the vault to complete Rumania's most successful-ever championship.

At Montreal in 1976, the Russia-Rumania rivalry was renewed and although Russia took the team gold with 390.35 marks to Rumania's silver medal-winning 387.15, the standard of competition was quite breathtaking and this was reflected in the marking which although from time to time veering towards the over-generous with an almost embarrassingly large number of perfect 10 scores, still provided fair reward for the outstandingly high level of competition. The leading light, of course, was Comaneci with a total of seven perfect scores in her

individual and team exercises. Her performances lacked some of the charm of Korbut, the spellbinder of 1972, but her poise, confidence and, above all, her technical perfection — especially her daring Radochla somersault on the bars — made her near-unstoppable. Unplaced in the vault, where Kim and Tourischeva took gold and silver, Comaneci won a bronze in the floor exercises — behind the same Russian pair — and then took the gold medal in the beam and the bars, scoring a hitherto "impossible" score of 20. It was really her performance in this discipline that gave Comaneci her combined gold as can be seen from the scores of the first three: Comaneci 79.275; Kim 78.675; Tourischeva 78.625. With just 0.65 of a mark — measured perhaps in terms of a microsecond of hesitation — separating the top three girls, the competition clearly could not have been any closer. Although Rumania's other top gymnast Teodora Ungureanu competed nobly to win a silver in the bars and a bronze in the beam, the Games really belonged to Comaneci who eclipsed Korbut, winning the combined gold.

In 1977 at the European Championships, Comaneci again won the combined gold ahead of yet another "new" Russian — Elena Moukhina and the ever-reliable Nelli Kim. To that victory was added gold in the bars and silver in the vault, but to many observers Comaneci's performances had lost just a little "something" and this

view was confirmed by her performance during the 1978 World Championships in Strasbourg where she could only finish in overall fourth place behind a Russian clean-sweep of Moukhina, Kim and Natalia Shaposhnikova. However with Emilia Eberle one place behind Comaneci and Marilena Neacsu finishing 14th, Rumania still took the team silver, though their final total of 384.25 was a sizeable — in gymnastic terms — 4.5 marks behind the victorious Russians.

Above
Nadia Comaneci caught in typical flowing motion during her prime speciality event – the asymmetric bars. Her perfect 20 points score for this event in Montreal may never be equalled.

Below
Second to Comaneci on the bars at Montreal, Teodora Ungureanu was another who helped Rumania to the team silver behind Russia. She also won a bronze on the beam – behind Comaneci's gold – at the Olympiad.

U.S.A.

If any nation is likely to emerge over the next few years as a serious challenger to the virtual world gymnastics monopoly currently enjoyed by the Soviet Union and Japan, it could well turn out to be the United States — a country that has made remarkable strides over the past few years in the build-up to hosting the 1982 World Championships.

In the post-war era, the U.S.A. did not win a medal in any World or Olympic tournament until the World Championships of 1970 when Cathy Rigby — now a renowned television commentator on gymnastics — won a silver on the beam behind Zuchold of East Germany who finished just 0.15 of a point ahead. First blood to the American girls then, but the men had to wait for their first success with Peter Kormann's bronze medal in the floor exercises at the 1976 Montreal Olympics, behind the Russians Andrianov and Marchenko.

In the 1978 World Championships, though, the Americans really came to the fore with some sterling performances from both men and women competitors. In the team classification, the men finished in fourth position behind Japan, Russia and East Germany and created quite an upset by pushing the strong West Germans into fifth place. The margin between East Germany and the Americans was 3.05 marks, which is quite a gap in gymnastic terms, but nevertheless one which must have caused one or two uneasy moments in the East German camp as the competition progressed.

The American girls fared slightly less well in the team event than their male counterparts by finishing in fifth position—the highest achieved by any Western nation — behind Russia, Rumania, East Germany and Hungary. The points gap between the U.S.A. and the Hungarian girls was just 0.6 of a mark, but the bronze medal-winning East Germans were nearly five points clear of that total, while the gap between the States and Russia was in the order of 11 points—a truly massive margin.

Individually, the Americans really asserted themselves at Strasbourg. Of the men, Kurt Thomas finished sixth overall, with Bart Connor in ninth place and Mike Wilson a little further down the list at 20th. Thomas's 9.80 in the floor exercises was only bettered by the 9.85 of overall champion Andrianov and a similar 9.80 in that same discipline was registered by Mike Wilson. Bart Connor came up with another 9.80 — this time in the pommel horse — a score that only the brilliant Hungarian Zoltan Magyar could top — and although the Americans scored poorly on the rings, Kurt Thomas, along with several other competitors, was just 0.05 of a mark behind Andrianov's 9.85 in the vault and 0.1 of a mark behind a third Andrianov 9.85 on the high bar.

Of the American women, Kathy Johnson and Rhonda Schwandt finished eighth and ninth respectively, while Marcia Frederick — in common with Mike Wilson — finished 20th. (The placing of the Americans, incidentally, of sixth, ninth and 20th for the men and eighth, ninth and 20th for the women indicates a remarkably consistent development in both the men's and women's sides of the sport in the U.S.A. which could augur extremely well for the future.)

In common with the men, Johnson, Schwandt and Frederick turned in some excellent performances: Schwandt's 9.85 in the floor exercises was only bettered by the 9.9 of Moukhina, Kim and Comaneci and while the two Russians again scored 9.9s on the bars, their performance was equalled by Marcia Frederick. After poor showings on the beam, with just 9.25 for Johnson, 9.05 for Schwandt and 9.0 for Frederick in comparison to Nelli Kim's dazzling 9.9, Kathy Johnson recovered with a 9.9 in the floor exercises — just 0.05 of a mark behind the inevitable Russian duo of Moukhina and Kim.

Left
Marcia Frederick, the current World Champion on the asymmetric bars. The Americans, with excellent recent performances, seem to be on the brink of establishing themselves as a real force in the world of gymnastics.

With their improvement in the Seventies bringing them to the very fringes of top international honours, America's flourishing youth development programme should stand them in good stead for Moscow in 1980 and, more importantly, for the 1982 World Championships which *could* be the tournament at which — individual performances notwithstanding — the Americans arrive as a team to challenge Japan, Russia and East Germany in the men's events and Russia, Rumania and East Germany in the women's. With their fine national facilities and, most importantly, their unrivalled expertise in promoting gymnastics within their schooling system, the Americans have at least laid the foundations for the future.

And who, in addition to the likes of Thomas, Connor, Wilson, Johnson, Schwandt and Frederick, will be the gymnasts to represent the U.S.A. in future competition? Of the established members of the side, Thomas and the dynamic Bart Connor appear to be certainties for Moscow while James Hartung is a youngster who could also feature strongly.

Of the girls, Kathy Johnson is on the very edge of top world class, while Marcia Frederick, who, but for a disastrous performance on the beam in Strasbourg, might have been challenging the medal positions, is even now one of the top competitors in the world on the asymmetric bars. As she is still in her early teens, who is to say that Marcia Frederick in Moscow might not be the successor to Olga Korbut in Munich and Nadia Comaneci in Montreal? Another to watch is Donna Turnbow who won the 1978 "Champions All" event in London, while graduates from junior ranks could include Merilyn Chapman, winner of the individual title at the first British World Invitation event, Kelly McCoy and Jackie Cassello. Since Rhonda Schwandt, who performed with such distinction at Strasbourg, is a former member of the U.S.A. national junior team, the standard is obviously extremely high.

Perhaps the Americans lack the iron determination and discipline of their Eastern European counterparts, but if their will to win is anything to go by, they could become a very potent world force.

Above left
Although not having America's potential in depth, Canada are nevertheless the best Commonwealth gymnastics nation. When gymnastics was introduced to the Commonwealth Games for the first time at Edmonton in 1978, Canada won both men's and women's team gold and the individual combined golds. Karen Kelsall, here seen on the beam, was 17th overall at the World Championships in 1978.

Above right
Mike Wilson, one of the outstanding young American gymnasts who has just come to the fore and who will play a vital role in the United States' Olympic challenge in Moscow.

Basic Gymnastics

The first moves for all gymnasts

The development of gymnastics over the past decade has been remarkable and the sport is booming as never before. For the many people who have accepted the challenge of gymnastics a revolution has occurred affecting their social and physical way of life. To the layman or even the gymnasts themselves, the sport offers a confusing yet exciting picture. It has not been intended that this book should be a coaching manual nor to explain how gymnastic skills are acquired, such a book would demand many volumes. Nevertheless on the following pages are shown just a few of the skills, with the exception of the vault, which make up the ten Olympic disciplines — four for women, six for men. On each, only the elementary movements are demonstrated, however, most gymnastic programmes lend themselves to amazingly acrobatic skills, especially the women's floor where the pace of the routine is guided by the tempo of the accompanying music. The rings and the pommel horse are exclusively men's exercises requiring an enormous amount of strength and stamina in order to maintain the grace of the movements. The women's

alternative to these two is the beam, equally representative of strength and stamina. Asymmetric bars are designed for women while the men have the horizontal bar and the parallel bars — the bars often being the source of some of the most spectacular and exciting sequences in modern gymnastics.

All gymnastic skills, even the most complex are a development of elementary body movements. A Rodochla somersault between the bars is a development of the forward somersault, which in turn is developed from the most simple and basic of all movements — a forward roll. Each must first be learned then practised to perfection before the next step is attempted. The first and most important lesson a young gymnast can learn is, having acquired a skill, to perfect it and to go on perfecting it.

A gymnast's repertoire consists mainly of three grades of skills — elementary, medium, and advanced. The elementary and medium skills should be practised incessantly in order that they become almost a subconscious effort, thus permitting all concentration to be directed towards the exercises' maximum skill areas.

Left
Steffi Kraker, on the vault.

MENS PARALLEL BARS

MENS FLOOR

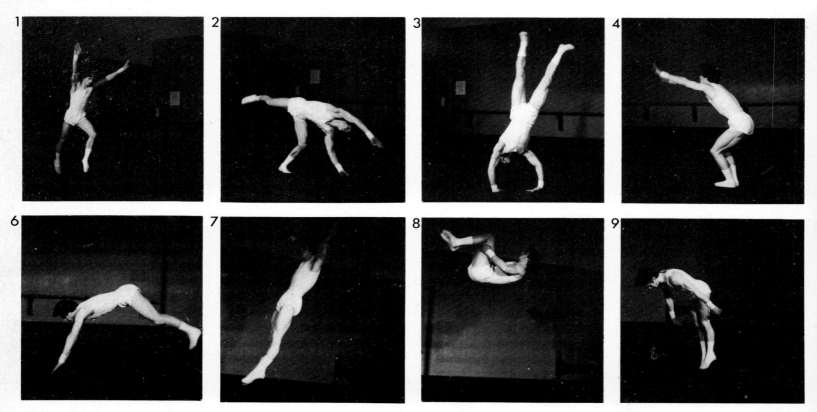

Parallel Bars

As with Pommels, Rings and Horizontal bar exercises, correct swinging is paramount. Here are two short elements showing swing and strength.

 1 *Hold starting position*
 2 *smoothly into pike position*
 3 *then through to handstand,*
 4 *handstand complete.*
 5 *Alternatively, backward and*
 6 *forward swinging*
 7 *lift body and complete handstand*
 8 *change hands and twist body*
 9 *downward swing*
10 *to begin tumbling dismount*
11 *full somersault*
12 *perfect landing*

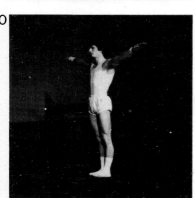

Men's Floor

The men's exercise differs from the women's by virtue of added strength balances and more acrobatics, also of course, there is no music accompaniment.

The round off back flip back somersault

 1 *The step into*
 2 *round off*
 3 *push off hands into*
 4 *take off*
 5 *flip*
 6 *push off hands*
 7 *take off – straight jump*
 8 *tuck back somersault*
 9 *stretching legs for*
10 *a perfect landing*

MENS HIGH BAR

MENS RINGS

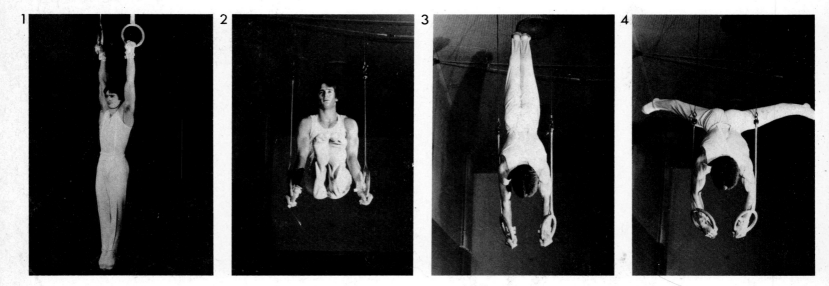

Horizontal Bar (high bar)

Just as leg circles are the basis of good pommel horse work, so grand circles or giant swings are the basis of good horizontal bar swinging and they predominate in any bar exercise.

1 *Swing,*

2 *a backward fly away, back away.*

3 *Note backward circle is where the chest is leading*

4 *Hence the chest leads in a backward dismount.*

5 *Landing.*

6 *During upward swing,*

7 *during downward swing.*

8 *The grand circle. Body extended fully,*

9 *exaggerated shortening of swinging radius,*

10 *dismount.*

Rings

A complete ring exercise must contain swinging, strength and held balance skills.

1 *All exercises start here – the hang.*

2 *Now the strength element,*

3 *swing up to hand stand,*

4 *slowly lowered down,*

5 *To half lever straddle. This being the held position.*

MENS POMMEL HORSE

1

2

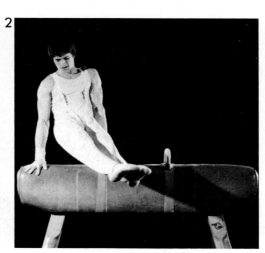

3

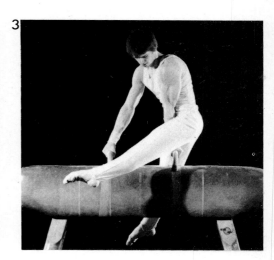

7

8

WOMENS FLOOR

The floor exercise gives unlimited scope to introduce acrobatic skills. Here are two skills, a free walkover and a splits leap.

1

2

3

4

Pommel Horse

1 Double leg circles, hands on pommels. Leg circles are the cornerstone of the exercise.

2 Legs still together, travel to end of horse.

3 Back to pommels, a feint swing of leg, to right then to left.

4, 5 Scissors, without which no exercise is complete; right and left, forward and backward.

6, 7 A more recent and advanced development of scissors, the "flares".

8 Back to double leg circles on end of horse.

9 Dismount.

Floor

1 The step into the take off.

2 The take off foot drive is evident.

3 These three pictures show the

4 mid positions with legs

5 almost in splits,

6 the landing with an immediate

7 step into a pose position.

WOMENS ASYMMETRIC BARS

Asymmetric Bars

1 *Starting position standing on low bar*

2 *splits handstand,*

3 *fully extended into dismount*

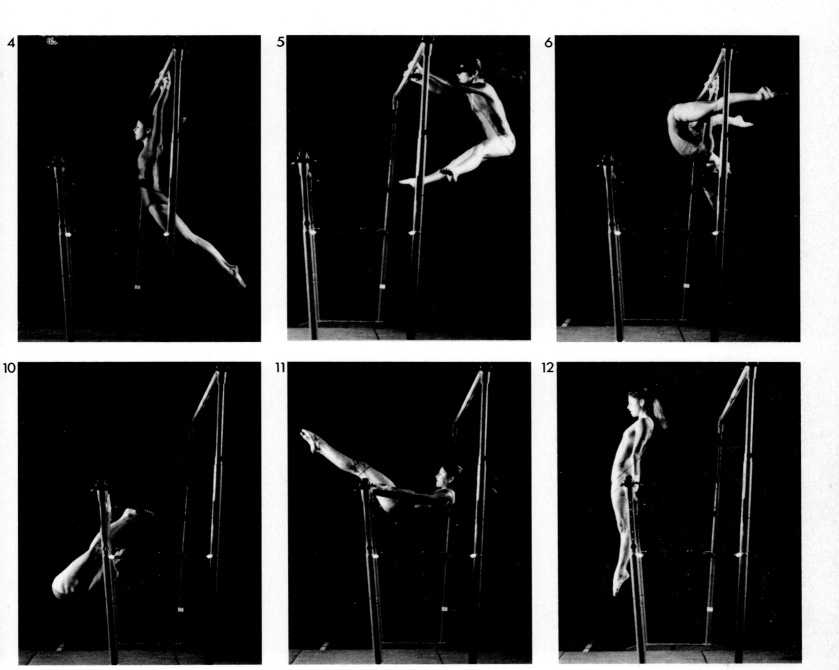

Asymmetric Bars
The following elements on the uneven asymmetric bars are from the Olympic compulsory exercise.

1 *Long underswing, upstart to catch high bar*

2 *extended under the bar*

3 *gaining momentum*

4 *back on to higher bar*

5 *backward somersault beginning*

6 *in straddle piked position*

7 *tumble turn –*

8 *catch low bar*

9 *long underswing*

10 *passing straight leap between hands (stoop)*

11 *rise into*

12 *back support on low bar*

WOMENS BEAM

Beam
*Two short sequences of
typical beam elements*

1 *Starting position,*

2 *into backward walkover.*

3 *Backward walkover*

4 *onto toe balance then to*

5 *sitting position,*

6 *to stand*

7 *then step into cartwheel,*

8, 8a *to stag handstand*

9 *step out of stag balance*

10 *into pose.*

1 *Standing pose to*

2 *needle stand*

3 *step forward, swing leg
forward*

4 *right leg down towards beam*

5 *bend backwards into bridge*

Competitions and Results

The roll of honour

MEN'S EUROPEAN CHAMPIONSHIPS

Combined exercises	Vault	Pommels	P Bars	Floor
FRANKFURT 1955				
SHAKHLIN Boris *U*	DICKHUT Adalbert *G*	SHAKHLIN Boris *U*	AZARIAN Albert *U*	PROROK Vladimir *C*
AZARIAN Albert *U*			SHAKHLIN Boris *U*	
BANTZ Helmut *G*			BANTZ Helmut *G*	
PARIS 1957				
BLUME Jo Sp	TITOV Yuri *U*	BLUME Jo Sp	[GUNTHARD Jack *Sw*	THORESSON William *Swed*
TITOV Yuri *U*	CSANYI Raymond *H*	BENKER Max *SW*	[BLUME Jo *Sp*	STUART Nik *GB*
BENKER Max *SW*	THORESSON William *Swed*	CAKLEC Ivan *Y*	BENKER Max *Sw*	SCHMITT Herbert *G*
COPENHAGEN 1959				
TITOV Yuri *U*	[TITOV Yuri *U*	TITOV Yuri *U*	TITOV Yuri *U*	FIVIAN Ernst *S*
STOLBOV Pavel *U*	[THORESSON William *Swed*	ECKMANN Eugen *Fin*	DANIS Ferdinand *Cz*	THORESSON William *Swed*
FURST Philip *G*	FIVIAN Ernst *S*	FURST Philip *G*	STOLBOV Pavel *U*	TITOV Yuri *U*
LUXEMBOURG 1961				
CERAR Miroslav *Y*	CARMINUCCI Giovanni *I*	CERAR Miroslav *Y*	CERAR Miroslav *Y*	MENICHELLI Franco *I*
TITOV Yuri *U*	MENICHELLI Franco *I*	[FURST Philip *G*	LEONTIEV Victor *U*	LEONTIEV Victor *U*
CARMINUCCI Giovanni *I*	CERAR Miroslav *Y*	[LEONTIEV Victor *U*	[CARMINUCCI Giovanni *I*	CERAR Miroslav *Y*
	FIVIAN Ernst *Sw*		[MENICHELLI Franco *I*	
	THORESSON W. *Swed*			
BELGRADE 1963				
CERAR Miroslav *Y*	KRBEC Premysil *Cz*	CERAR Miroslav *Y*	CARMINUCCI Giovanni *I*	MENICHELLI Franco *I*
SHAKHLIN Boris *U*	CERAR Miroslav *Y*	KERDEMELIDI Vladimir *U*	SHAKHLIN Boris *U*	KERDEMELIDI Vladimir *U*
KERDEMELIDI Vladimir *U*	[STROT Martin *Y*	SHAKHLIN Boris *U*	MENICHELLI Franco *I*	CERAR Miroslav *Y*
	[KERDEMELIDI Vladimir *U*			
ANTWERP 1965				
MENICHELLI Franco *I*	LISITSKI Victor *U*	LISITSKI Victor *U*	CERAR Miroslav *Y*	MENICHELLI Franco *I*
LISITSKI Victor *U*	[ADAMOV Gueorgui *B*	CERAR Miroslav *Y*	MENICHELLI Franco *I*	[CERAR Miroslav *Y*
DIAMIDOV Serguei *U*	[HEINONEN Raimo *F*	DIAMIDOV Serguei *U*	DIAMIDOV Serguei *U*	[LISITSKI Victor *U*
	STORHAUG Age *N*	[LAIHO Olli *F*	KOPPE Erwin *DDR*	
TAMPERE 1967				
VORONIN Mikhail *U*	LISITSKY Victor *U*	VORONIN Mikhail *U*	VORONIN Mikhail *U*	LAINE Lasse *Fin*
LISITSKY Victor *U*	ADAMOV Gueorgui *B*	CERAR Miroslav *Y*	MENICHELLI Franco *I*	MENICHELLI Franco *I*
MENICHELLI Franco *I*	DIETRICH Gerhard *DDR*	DIETRICH Gerhard *DDR*	CARMINUCCI Giovanni *I*	KUBICA Nicolai *P*
WARSAW 1969				
VORONIN Mikhail *U*	KLIMENKO Victor *U*	CERAR Miroslav *Y*	VORONIN Mikhail *U*	CHRISTOW Raytche *B*
KLIMENKO Victor *U*	[KUBICA Nicolai *P*	KUBICA Wilhelm *P*	[CERAR Miroslav *Y*	LISITSKY Victor *U*
KUBICA Nicolai *P*	[VORONIN Mikhail *U*	VORONIN Mikhail *U*	[KLIMENKO Victor *U*	KUBICA Sylwester *P*
MADRID 1971				
KLIMENKO Victor *U*	ANDRIANOV Nikolai *U*	ANDRIANOV Nikolai *U*	CARMINUCCI Giovanni *I*	CHRISTOV Raytche *B*
VORONIN Mikhail *U*	SZAJNA Andrzej *P*	BREHME Matthias *DDR*	[ANDRIANOV Nikolai *U*	GINES Jose *Sp*
ANDRIANOV Nikolai *U*	KOSTE Klaus *DDR*	VORONIN Mikhail *U*	[KOSTE Klaus *DDR*	ANDRIANOV Nikolai *U*
			[VORONIN Mikhail *U*	
GRENOBLE 1973				
KLIMENKO Victor *U*	ANDRIANOV Nikolai *U*	MAGYAR Zoltan *H*	KLIMENKO Victor *U*	ANDRIANOV Nikolai *U*
ANDRIANOV Nikolai *U*	SZAJNA Andrzej *P*	KUBICA Wilhelm *P*	ANDRIANOV Nikolai *U*	KLIMENKO Victor *U*
KOSTE Klaus *DDR*	MOLNAR Imre *H*	KLIMENKO Victor *U*	NISSINEN Mauno *Fin*	KOSTE Klaus *DDR*
BERNE 1975				
ANDRIANOV Nikolai *U*	ANDRIANOV Nikolai *U*	MAGYAR Zoltan *H*	ANDRIANOV Nikolai *U*	[ANDRIANOV Nikolai *U*
GIENGER Eberhard *BRD*	SZAJNA Andrzej *P*	ANDRIANOV Nikolai *U*	DETIATIN Alexandre *U*	[SZAJNA Andrzej *P*
DETIATIN Alexandre *U*	TABAK Jiri *Cz*	GIENGER Eberhard *BRD*	KLIMENKO Victor *U*	TABAK Jiri *Cz*
VILNIUS 1977				
MARKELOV Vladimir *U*	[TABAK Jiri *Cz*	MAGYAR Zoltan *H*	TIKHONOV Vladimir *U*	TKACHEV Alexandre *U*
TKACHEV Alexandre *U*	[BARTHEL Ralph *DDR*	NIKOLAI Michael *DDR*	[BARTHEL Ralph *DDR*	MARKELOV Vladimir *U*
TIKHONOV Vladimir *U*	MARKELOV Vladimir *U*	MARKELOV Vladimir *U*	[GIENGER Eberhard *BRD*	TIKHONOV Vladimir *U*

Right
*Russia's greatest all-rounder of recent
years, Nikolai Andrianov caught in
mid-vault. He won four gold medals at the
European championships in 1975, for
parallel bars, vault, floor and combined
exercises.*

Rings	H Bar
AZARIAN Albert *U*	SHAKHLIN Boris *U*
BLUME Jo *Sp* TITOV Yuri *U* SUOMENI Kalevi *Fin*	GUNTHARD Jack *Sw* BLUME Jo *Sp* TITOV Yuri *U*
TITOV Yuri *U* STOLBOV Pavel *U* KAPSAZOV Velik *B* KESTOLA Otto *Fin*	STOLBOV Pavel *U* TITOV Yuri *U* [CRONSTEDT Jean *Swed* KESTOLA Otto *Fin*
CERAR Miroslav *Y* KAPSAZOV Velik *B* TITOV Yuri *U*	TITOV Yuri *U* CSANYI Raymond *H* KESTOLA Otto *Fin*
CERAR Miroslav *Y* SHAKHLIN Boris *U* KAPSAZOV Velik *B*	[SHAKHLIN Boris *U* CERAR Miroslav *Y* KERDEMELIDI Vladimir *U*
LISITSKI Victor *U* MENICHELLI Franco *I* CERAR Miroslav *Y*	MENICHELLI Franco *I* LISITSKI Victor *U* DIAMIDOV Serguei *U*
VORONIN Mikhail *U* LISITSKY Victor *U* KUBICA Nicolai *P*	LISITSKY Victor *U* VORONIN Mikhail *U* [CERAR Miroslav *P* MENICHELLI Franco *I*
VORONIN Mikhail *U* KUBICA Nicolai *P* KLIMENKO Victor *U*	[LISITSKI Victor *U* KLIMENKO Victor *U* CERAR Miroslav *Y*
VORONIN Mikhail *U* ANDRIANOV Nikolai *U* SZAJNA Andrej *P*	KOSTE Klaus *DDR* VORONIN Mikhail *U* HURZELER Roland *S*
KLIMENKO Victor *U* ANDRIANOV Nikolai *U* GRECU Dan *R*	[GIENGER Eberhard *BRD* KOSTE Klaus *DDR* THUNE Wolfgang *DDR*
GRECU Dan *R* BORS Mihai *R* DETIATIN Alexandre *U*	[GIENGER Ebehard *BRD* ANDRIANOV Nikolai *U* SZAJNA Andrzej *P*
MARKELOV Vladimir *U* TKACHEV Alexandre *U* TIKHONOV Vladimir *U*	DELTCHEV Stojan *B* [MARKELOV Vladimir *U* TKACHEV Alexandre *U*

WOMEN'S EUROPEAN CHAMPIONSHIPS

Individual	Vault	Bars	Beam	Floor
BUCHAREST 1957				
LATYNINA Larissa *U*	LATYNINA Larissa *U*	LATYNINA Larissa *U*	LATYNINA Larissa *U*	LATYNINA Larissa *U*
TEODORESCU Elena *R*	MANINA Tamara *U*	TEODORESCU Elena *R*	IOVAN Sonia *R*	TEODORESCU Elena *R*
IOVAN Sonia *R*	IOVAN Sonia *R*	BOSOKOVA Eva *Cz*	MANINA Tamara *U*	BOSOKOVA Eva *Cz*
KRAKOW, POLAND 1959				
KOT Natalie *P*	KOT Natalie *P*	ASTAKHOVA Polina *U*	CASLAVSKA Vera *Cz*	ASTAKHOVA Polina *U*
TEODORESCU Elena *R*	CASLAVSKA Vera *Cz*	TEODORESCU Elena *R*	IOVAN Sonia *R*	MANINA Tamara *U*
IOVAN Sonia *R*	FOST Ingrid *DDR*	FOST Ingrid *DDR*	KOT Nelli *P*	BOSOKOVA Eva *Cz*
LEIPZIG 1961				
LATYNINA Larissa *U*	STARK Ute *DDR*	ASTAKHOVA Polina *U*	ASTAKHOVA Polina *U*	LATYNINA Larissa *U*
ASTAKHOVA Polina *U*	FOST Ingrid *DDR*	LATYNINA Lakissa *U*	LATYNINA Larissa *U*	ASTAKHOVA Polina *U*
[CASLAVSKA Vera *Cz*	KOT Natalie *P*	FOST Ingrid *DDR*	FOST Ingrid *DDR*	CASLAVSKA Vera *Cz*
FOST Ingrid *DDR*				
PARIS 1963				
BILIC Mirjana *Y*	EGMAN Solveig *Swed*	BELMER Thea *Hol*	RYDELL Eva *Swed*	BILIC Mirjana *Y*
EGMAN Solveig *Swed*	BELMER Thea *Hol*	KOCIS Kosanji *Y*	KOCIS Kosanji *Y*	EGMAN Solveig *Swed*
RYDELL Eva *Swed*	VIERSTA Jannie *Hol*	EGMAN Solveig *Swed*	BILIC Solveig *Y*	KOCIS Kosanji *Y*
SOFIA 1965				
CASLAVSKA Vera *CZ*	CASLAVSKA Vera *Cz*	CASLAVSKA Vera *Cz*	CASLAVSKA Vera *Cz*	CASLAVSKA Vera *Cz*
LATYNINA Larissa *U*	STARK Ute *DDR*	LATYNINA Larissa *U*	LATYNINA Larissa *U*	LATYNINA Larissa *U*
RADOCHLA Brigit *DDR*	LATYNINA Larissa *U*	KARASCHKA Maria *B*	[RADOCHLA Brigit *DDR*	[RADOCHLA Brigit *DDR*
			PETRIK L. *U*	
AMSTERDAM 1967				
CASLAVSKA Vera *Cz*	CASLAVSKA Vera *Cz*	CASLAVSKA Vera *Cz*	CASLAVSKA Vera *Cz*	CASLAVSKA Vera *Cz*
DRUGININA Zinaida *U*	ZUCHOLD Erika *DDR*	JANZ Karin *DDR*	KUCHINSKAYA Natalia *U*	KUCHINSKAYA Natalia *U*
KRAYCIROVAJ Maria *Cz*	JANZ Karin *DDR*	KRAYCIROVAJ Maria *Cz*	DRUGININA Zinaida *U*	DRUGININA Zinaida *U*
LANDSKRONA 1969				
JANZ Karin *DDR*	JANZ Karin *DDR*	JANZ Karin *DDR*	JANZ Karin *DDR*	KARASSOVA Olga *U*
KARASSOVA Olga *U*	ZUCHOLD Erika *DDR*	KARASSOVA Olga *U*	KARASSOVA Olga *U*	JANZ Karin *DDR*
[TOURISCHEVA Ludmila *U*	KARASSOVA Olga *U*	TOURISCHEVA Ludmila *U*	KOSTALOVA Jindra *Cz*	[KOSTALOVA Jindra *Cz*
ZUCHOLD Erika *DDR*				TOURISCHEVA Ludmila *U*
MINSK 1971				
[TOURISCHEVA Ludmila *U*	TOURISCHEVA Ludmila *U*	LAZAKOVITCH Tamara *U*	LAZAKOVITCH Tamara *U*	TOURISCHEVA Ludmila *U*
LAZAKOVITCH Tamara *U*	LAZAKOVITCH Tamara *U*	TOURISCHEVA Ludmila *U*	TOURISCHEVA Ludmila *U*	LAZAKOVITCH Tamara *U*
ZUCHOLD Erika *DDR*	ZUCHOLD Erika *DDR*	HELLMANN Angelika *DDR*	ZUCHOLD Erika *DDR*	ZUCHOLD Erika *DDR*
LONDON 1973				
TOURISCHEVA Ludmila *U*	[HELLMANN Angelika *DDR*	TOURISCHEVA Ludmila *U*	TOURISCHEVA Ludmila *U*	TOURISCHEVA Ludmila *U*
KORBUT Olga *U*	TOURISCHEVA Ludmila *U*	HELLMANN Angelika *DDR*	GOREAC Alina *R*	GERSCHAU Kirstin *DDR*
GERSCHAU Kirstin *DDR*	SCHORN Ute *BDR*	GOREAC Alina *R*	GRIGORAS Anca *R*	GOREAC Alina *R*
SKIEN, NORWAY 1975				
COMANECI Nadia *R*	COMANECI Nadia *R*	COMANECI Nadia *R*	COMANECI Nadia *R*	KIM Nelli *U*
KIM Nelli *U*	SCHMEISSER Richarda *DDR*	ZINKE Annelore *DDR*	KIM Nelli *U*	COMANECI Nadia *R*
ZINKE Annelore *DDR*	[GOREAC Alina *R*	KIM Nelli *U*	GOREAC Alina *R*	TOURISCHEVA Ludmila *U*
	KIM Nelli *U*			
PRAGUE 1977				
COMANECI Nadia *R*	KIM Nelli *U*	[MOUKHINA Elena *U*	MOUKHINA Elena *U*	[MOUKHINA Elena *U*
MOUKHINA Elena *U*	COMANECI Nadia *R*	COMANECI Nadia *R*	KIM Nelli *U*	FILATOVA Maria *U*
KIM Nelli *U*	MOUKHINA Elena *U*	KRAKER Steffi *DDR*	FILATOVA Maria *U*	KIM Nelli *U*

Left
Nelli Kim, who has taken over the mantle of Korbut and Tourischeva and will head Russia's bid for gold in the Moscow Olympic Games. She makes up a formidable quartet with Elena Moukhina, Natalia Shaposhnikova and Maria Filatova.

Right
Sure-handed Elena Moukhina on the asymmetric bars. She took the overall World Women's title in 1978, to follow a double Gold in the World Cup the year before.

WORLD CHAMPIONSHIPS

BASLE, SWITZERLAND 1950
MEN

Team	Individual	Floor	Pommels	Rings
SWITZERLAND	LEHMANN Walter *Sw*	STALDER Joseph *Sw*	STALDER Joseph *Sw*	LEHMANN Walter *Sw*
FINLAND	ADATTE Marcel *Sw*	GEBENDINGER Ernst *Sw*	ADATTE Marcel *Sw*	ROVE Olavi *Fin*
FRANCE	ROVE Olavi *F*	DOT Raymond *F*	LEHMANN Walter *Sw*	EUGSTER Hans *Sw*

WOMEN

Team	Individual	Floor	Beam	Vault
SWEDEN	RAKOCZY Helena *P*	RAKOCZY Helena *P*	RAKOCZY Helena *P*	RAKOCZY Helena *P*
FRANCE	PETERSEN Gota *Swed*	KOCIS Tereza *Y*	NUTTI Maria *I*	KOLAR Gertchen *A*
ITALY	KOLAR Gertchen *A*	REINDLOWA Stefania *P*	MACCHINI Licia *I*	LEMOINE Alexandrine *F*

ROME 1954
MEN

Team	Individual	Floor	Pommels	Rings
USSR	MURATOV Valentin *U*	MURATOV Valentin *U*	SHAGWYAN Grant *U*	AZARIAN Albert *U*
JAPAN	CHUKARIN Victor *U*	TAKEMOTO Masho *J*	STALDER Joseph *Sw*	KOROLKOV Eugene *U*
SWITZERLAND	SHAGWYAN Grant *U*	THORESSON William *Swed*	CHUKARIN Victor *U*	MURATOV Valentin *U*

WOMEN

Team	Individual	Floor	Beam	Vault
USSR	ROUDIKO Galina *U*	MANINA Tamara *U*	TANAKA Keiko *J*	MANINA Tamara *U*
HUNGARY	BOSOKOVA Eva *Cz*	BOSOKOVA Eva *Cz*	BOSOKOVA Eva *Cz*	PETTERSON Anna *Swed*
CZECHOSLOVAKIA	RAKOCZY Helena *P*	GOROKHOVSKAYA Maria *U*	KELETI Agnes *H*	BERGREN Evy *Swed*

MOSCOW 1958
MEN

Team	Individual	Floor	Pommels	Rings
USSR	SHAKHLIN Boris *U*	TAKEMOTO Masao *J*	SHAKHLIN Boris *U*	AZARIAN Albert *U*
JAPAN	ONO Takashi *J*	ONO Takashi *J*	STOLBOV Pavel *U*	AIHARA Noboyuki *J*
CZECHOSLOVAKIA	TITOV Yuri *U*	TITOV Yuri *U*	CERAR Miroslav *Y*	TITOV Yuri *U*

WOMEN

Team	Individual	Floor	Beam	Vault
USSR	LATYNINA Larissa *U*	BOSOKOVA Eva *Cz*	LATYNINA Larissa *U*	LATYNINA Larissa *U*
CZECHOSLOVAKIA	BOSOKOVA Eva *Cz*	LATYNINA Larissa *U*	MURATOVA Sofia *U*	MURATOVA Sofia *U*
RUMANIA	MANINA Tamara *U*	TONAKA Keiko *J*	TONAKA Keiko *J*	KALINA Lidia *U*
				MANINA Tamara *U*

PRAGUE 1962
MEN

Team	Individual	Floor	Pommels	Rings
JAPAN	TITOV Yuri *U*	AIHARA Nobuyuki *J*	CERAR Miroslav *Y*	TITOV Yuri *U*
USSR	ENDO Yukio *J*	ENDO Yukio *J*	SHAKHLIN Boris *U*	ENDO Yukio *J*
CZECHOSLOVAKIA	SHAKHLIN Boris *U*	MENICHELLI Franco *I*	MITSUKURI Takashi *J*	SHAKHLIN Boris *U*
			YU LIEH-FENG *China*	

WOMEN

Team	Individual	Floor	Beam	Vault
USSR	LATYNINA Larissa *U*	LATYNINA Larissa *U*	BOSOKOVA Eva *CZ*	CASLAVSKA Vera *Cz*
CZECHOSLOVAKIA	CASLAVSKA Vera *Cz*	PERVUSCHINA Irina *U*	LATYNINA Larissa *U*	LATYNINA Larissa *U*
JAPAN	PERVUSCHINA Irina *U*	CASLAVSKA Vera *Cz*	IKEDA Keiko *J*	MANINA Tamara *U*
			DUCZA Aniko *H*	

DORTMUND 1966
MEN

Team	Individual	Floor	Pommels	Rings
JAPAN	VORONIN Mikhail *U*	NAKAYAMA Akinori *J*	CERAR Miroslav *Y*	VORONIN Mikhail *U*
USSR	TSURUMI Shuji *J*	ENDO Yukio *J*	VORONIN Mikhail *U*	NAKAYAMA Akinori *J*
DDR	NAKAYAMA Akinori *J*	MENICHELLI Franco *I*	KATO Takashi *J*	MENICHELLI Franco *I*

WOMEN

Team	Individual	Floor	Beam	Vault
CZECHOSLOVAKIA	CASLAVSKA Vera *Cz*	KUCHINSKAYA Natalia *U*	KUCHINSKAYA Natalia *U*	CASLAVSKA Vera *Cz*
USSR	KUCHINSIKAYA Natalia *U*	CASLAVSKA Vera *Cz*	CASLAVSKA Vera *Cz*	ZUCHOLD Erika *DDR*
JAPAN	IKEDA Kaiko *J*	DRUGININA Zinaida *U*	PETRIK Larissa *U*	KUCHINSKAYA Natalia *U*

LJUBLJANA, YUGOSLAVIA 1970
MEN

Team	Individual	Floor	Pommels	Rings
JAPAN	KENMOTSU Eizo *J*	NAKAYAMA Akinori *J*	CERAR Miroslav *Y*	NAKAYAMA Akinori *J*
USSR	TSUKAHARA Mitsuo *J*	KENMOTSU Eizo *J*	KENMOTSU Eizo *J*	TSUKUHARA Mitsuo *J*
DDR	NAKAYAMA Akinori *J*	KATO Takeshi *J*	KLIMENKO Victor *U*	VORONIN Mikhail *U*

WOMEN

Team	Individual	Floor	Beam	Vault
USSR	TOURISCHEVA Ludmila *U*	TOURISCHEVA Ludmila *U*	ZUCHOLD Erika *DDR*	ZUCHOLD Erika *DDR*
DDR	ZUCHOLD Erika *DDR*	KARASSOVA Olga *U*	RIGBY Cathy *USA*	JANZ Karin *DDR*
CZECHOSLOVAKIA	VORONINA Zinaida *U*	VORONINA Zinaida *U*	SCHMITT Christy *DDR*	TOURISCHEVA Ludmila *U*
			PETRIK Larissa *U.*	BURDA Ljubov *U*

VARNA, BULGARIA 1974
MEN

Team	Individual	Floor	Pommels	Rings
JAPAN	KASAMATSU Shigeru *J*	KASAMATSU Shigeru *J*	MAGYAR Zoltan *H*	ANDRIANOV Nikolai *U*
USSR	ANDRIANOV Nikolai *U*	KAJIYAMA Hiroshi *J*	ANDRIANOV Nikolai *U*	GRECU Dan *R*
DDR	KENMOTSU Eizo *J*	KERANOV Andrej *B*	KENMOTSU Eizo *J.*	SZAJNA Andrzej *P*

WOMEN

Team	Individual	Floor	Beam	Vault
USSR	TOURISCHEVA Ludmila *U*	TOURISCHEVA Ludmila *U*	TOURISCHEVA Ludmila *U*	KORBUT Olga *U*
DDR	KORBUT Olga *U*	KORBUT Olga *U*	KORBUT Olga *U*	TOURISCHEVA Ludmila *U*
HUNGARY	HELLMANN Angelika *DDR*	SAADI Elvira *U*	KIM Nelli *U*	PERDYKULOVA Bozena *Cz*
		SIHARULIDZE Rusuden *U*		

STRASBOURG, FRANCE 1978
MEN

Team	Individual	Floor	Pommels	Rings
JAPAN	ANDRIANOV Nikolai *U*	THOMAS Kurt *USA*	MAGYAR Zoltan *BRD*	ANDRIANOV Nikolai *U*
USSR	KENMOTSU Eizo *J*	KASAMATSU Shigeru *J*	DELTCHEV Stoian *B*	DETIATIN Alexandre *U*
DDR	KASAMATSU Shigeru *J*	DETIATIN Alexandre *U*	GIENGER Eberhard *BRD*	GRECU Dan *R*

WOMEN

Team	Individual	Floor	Beam	Vault
USSR	MOUKHINA Elena *U*	KIM Nelli *U*	COMANECI Nadia *R*	KIM Nelli *U*
RUMANIA	KIM Nelli *U*	MOUKHINA Elena *U*	MOUKHINA Elena *U*	COMANECI Nadia *R*
EAST GERMANY	SHAPOSHNIKOVA Natalia *U*	JOHNSON Kathy *USA*	EBERLE Emilia *R*	KRAKER Steffi *DDR*

* At this time women were in the process of changing from rings to asymmetric bars, and were therefore permitted during these championships to perform on either apparatus.

Vault
GEBENDINGER Ernst *Sw*
ROVE Olavi *Fin*
LEHMANN Walter *Sw*

P Bars
EUGSTER Hans *Sw*
ROVE Olavi *Fin*
DOT Raymond *F*

H Bar
AALTONEN Paavo *Fin*
HUHTANEN Vaiko *Fin*
LEHMANN Walter *Sw*
STALDER Joseph *Sw*

Asymmetric Bars or Rings*
KOLAR Gertchen *A*
PETERSEN Gota *Swed*
RAKOCZY Helena *P*

Vault
SOTORNIK Leo *C*
BANTZ Helmut *G*
DIAIANI Serguei *U*

P Bars
CHUKARIN Victor *U*
STALDER Joseph *Sw*
TAKEMOTO Masho *J*
EUGSTER Hans *SW*
BANTZ Helmut *G*

H Bar
MURATOV Valentin *U*
BANTZ Helmut *G*
SHAKHLIN Boris *U*

Bars
KELETI Agnes *H*
ROUDIKO Galina *U*
RAKOCZY Helena *P*

Vault
TITOV Yuri *U*
TAKEMOTO Masao *J*
ONO Takashi *J*

P Bars
SHAKHLIN Boris *U*
ONO Takashi *J*
STOLBOV Pavel *U*

H Bar
SHAKHLIN Boris *U*
AZARIAN Albert *U*
TITOV Yuri *U*
TAKEMOTO Masao *J*

Bars
LATYNINA Larissa *U*
BOSOKOVA Eva *Cz*
ASTAKHOVA Polina *U*

Vault
KRBEC Premysel *Cz*
YAMASHITA Haruhiro *J*
SHAKHLIN Boris *U*
ENDO Yukio *J*

P Bars
CERAR Miroslav *Y*
SHAKHLIN Boris *U*
ENDO Yukio *J*

H Bar
ONO Takashi *J*
ENDO Yukio *J*
STOLBOV Pavel *U*

Bars
PERVUSCHINA Irina *U*
BOSOKOVA Eva *Cz*
LATYNINA Larissa *U*

Vault
MATSUDA Haruhiro *J*
KATO Takashi *J*
NAKAYAMA Akinori *J*

P Bars
DIAMIDOV Serguei *U*
VORONIN Mikhail *U*
CERAR Miroslav *Y*

H Bar
NAKAYAMA Akinori *J*
ENDO Yukio *J*
MITSUKURI Takashi *J*

Bars
KUCHINSKAYA Natalia *U*
IKEDA Kaiko *J*
MITSUKURI Taniko *J*

Vault
TSUKUHARA Mitsuo *J*
KLIMENKO Victor *U*
KATO Takashi *J*

P Bars
NAKAYAMA Akinori *J*
KENMOTSU Eizo *J*
VORONIN Mikhail *U*

H Bar
KENMOTSU Eizo *J*
NAKAYAMA Akinori *J*
HAYATA Takuji *J*
KOSTE Klaus *DDR*

Bars
JANZ Karin *DDR*
TOURISCHEVA Ludmila *U*
VORONINA Zinaida *U*

Vault
KASAMATSU Shigeru *J*
ANDRIANOV Nikolai *U*
KAJIYAMA Hiroshi *J*

P Bars
KENMOTSU Eizo *J*
ANDRIANOV Nikolai *U*
MARCHENKO Vladimir *U*

H Bar
GIENGER Eberhard *BDR*
THUNE Wolfgang *DDR*
KENMOTSU Eizo *J*
SZAJNA Andrzej *P*

Bars
ZINKE Annelore *DDR*
KORBUT Olga *U*
TOURISCHEVA Ludmila *U*

Vault
SHIMIZU *J*
ANDRIANOV Nikolai *U*
BARTHEL Ralph *DDR*

P Bars
KENMOTSU Eizo *J*
ANDRIANOV Nikolai *U*
KAJIYAMA Hiroshi *J*

H Bar
KASAMATSU Shigeru *J*
GIENGER Eberhard *BDR*
DELTCHEV Stoian *Bulg*

Bars
FREDERICK Marcia *USA*
MOUKHINA Elena *U*
EBERLE Emilia *R*

Above
Erika Zuchold struck gold in the vault and beam exercises in the 1970 World's.

Above
Svetlana Grozdova during the Russian display in London.

OLYMPICS

LONDON 1948
MEN

Team	Individual	Floor	Pommels	Rings
FINLAND	HUHTANEN Vaikko *Fin*	PATAKI Ferencе *H*	HUHTANEN Vaikko *Fin*	FREI K. *Sw*
SWITZERLAND	LEHMANN Walter *Sw*	MOGYOROSI-KLENCS Janos *H*	AALTONEN Paavo *Fin*	REUSCH M. *Sw*
HUNGARY	AALTONEN Paayo *Fin*	RUZICKA Zdenek *Cz*	SAVOLAINEN Heikko *Fin*	RUZICKA Zdenek *Cz*
			ZANETTI Luigi *I*	
			FIGONE Guido *I*	

Awards were not made in the sections above for women. Only since Helsinki have women followed the same programme as men.

HELSINKI 1952
MEN

Team	Individual	Floor	Pommels	Rings
USSR	CHUKARIN Victor *U*	THORESSON Karl *Swed*	CHUKARIN Victor *U*	SHAGINYAN Grant *U*
SWITZERLAND	SHAGINYAN Grant *U*	UESAKO Tadao *J*	SHAGINYAN Grant *U*	CHUKARIN Victor *U*
FINLAND	STALDER Joseph *Sw*	JOKIEL Jerzy *P*	KOROLKOV Eugen *U*	EUGSTER Hans *Sw*
				LEONKIN Dimitri *U*

WOMEN

Team	Individual	Floor	Vault	Bars
USSR	GOROKHOVSKAYA Maria *U*	KELETI Agnes *H*	KALINCHUK Ekaterina *U*	KORONDI Margit *H*
HUNGARY	BORCHAROVA Nina *U*	GOROKHOVSKAYA Maria *U*	GOROKHOVSKAYA Maria *U*	GOROKHOVSKAYA Maria *U*
CZECHOSLOVAKIA	KORONDI Margit *H*	KORONDI Agnes *H*	MINAICHEVA Galina *U*	KELETI Agnes *H*

MELBOURNE 1956
MEN

Team	Individual	Floor	Pommels	Rings
USSR	CHUKARIN Victor *U*	MURATOV Valentin *U*	SHAKHLIN Boris *U*	AZARIAN Albert *U*
JAPAN	ONO Takashi *J*	CHUKARIN Victor *U*	ONO Takashi *J*	MURATOV Valentin *U*
FINLAND	TITOV Yuri *U*	THORESSON William *Swed*	CHUKARIN Victor *U*	KUBOTA Msami *J*
		AIHARA N. *J*		TAKEMOTO Masao *J*

WOMEN

Team	Individual	Floor	Vault	Bars
USSR	LATYNINA Larissa *U*	KELETI Agnes *H*	LATYNINA Larissa *U*	KELETI Agnes *H*
HUNGARY	KELETI Agnes *H*	LATYNINA Larissa *U*	MANINA Tamara *U*	LATYNINA Larissa *U*
RUMANIA	MURATOVA Sofia *U*	LEUSTEAN Elena *R*	COLLING A-S. *Swed*	MURATOVA Sofia *U*
			TASS O. *H*	

ROME 1960
MEN

Team	Individual	Floor	Pommels	Rings
JAPAN	SHAKHLIN Boris *U*	AIHARA Noboyuki *J*	EKMAN Eugen *F*	AZARIAN Albert *U*
USSR	ONO Takashi *J*	TITOV Yuri *U*	SHAKHLIN Boris *U* 1st	SHAKHLIN Boris *U*
ITALY	TITOV Yuri *U*	MENICHELLI Franco *I*	TSURUMI Shuji *J*	ONO Takashi *J*
				KAPSAZOV Y. *Bulg*

WOMEN

Team	Individual	Floor	Vault	Bars
USSR	LATYNINA Larissa *U*	LATYNINA Larissa *U*	NIKOLAEVA Margarith *U*	ASTAKHOVA Polina *U*
CZECHOSLOVAKIA	MURATOVA Sofia *U*	ASTAKHOVA Polina *U*	MURATOVA Sofia *U*	LATYNINA Larissa *U*
RUMANIA	ASTAKHOVA Polina *U*	LYUKHINA Tamara *U*	LATYNINA Larissa *U*	LYUKHINA Tamara *U*

TOKYO 1964
MEN

Team	Individual	Floor	Pommels	Rings
JAPAN	ENDO Yukio *J*	MENICHELLI Franco *I*	CERAR Miroslav *Y*	HAYATA Takuji *J*
USSR	TSURUMI Shuji *J*	LISITSKI Victor *U*	TSURUMI Shuji *J*	MENICHELLI Franco *I*
GDR	SHAKHLIN Boris *U*	ENDO Yukio *J*	TSAPENKO Yuri *U*	SHAKHLIN Boris *U*
	LISITSKI Victor *U*			

WOMEN

Team	Individual	Floor	Bars	Beam
USSR	CASLAVSKA Vera *Cz*	ATYNINA Larissa *U*	ASTAKHOVA Polina *U*	CASLAVSKA Vera *Cz*
CZECHOSLOVAKIA	LATYNINA Larissa *U*	ASTAKHOVA Polina *U*	MAKRAY Katalin *H*	MANINA Tamara *U*
JAPAN	ASTAKHOVA Polina *U*	JANOSI Ducza *H*	LATYNINA Larissa *U*	LATYNINA Larissa *U*

MEXICO 1968
MEN

Team	Individual	Floor	Pommels	Rings
JAPAN	KATO Sawao *J*	KATO Sawao *J*	CERAR Miroslav *Y*	NAKAYAMA Akinori *J*
USSR	VORONIN Mikhail *U*	NAKAYAMA Akinori *J*	LAIHO Olli *F*	VORONIN Mikhail *U*
DDR	NAKAYAMA Akinori *J*	KATO Takeshi *J*	VORONIN Mikhail *U*	KATO Sawao *J*

WOMEN

Team	Individual	Floor	Vault	Bars
USSR	CASLAVSKA Vera *Cz*	CASLAVSKA Vera *Ca*	CASLAVSKA Vera *Cz*	CASLAVSKA Vera *Cz*
CZECHOSLOVAKIA	VORONINA Zinaida *U*	PETRIK Larissa *U* 1st	ZUCHOLD Erika *DDR*	JANZ Karen *DDR*
DDR	KUCHINSKAYA Natalia *U*	KUCHINSKAYA Natalia *U*	VORONINA Zinaida *U*	VORONINA Zinaida *U*

MUNICH 1972
MEN

Team	Individual	Floor	Pommels	Rings
JAPAN	KATO Sawao *J*	ANDRIANOV Nikolai *U*	KLIMENKO Victor *U*	NAKAYAMA Akinori *J*
USSR	KENMOTSU Eizo *J*	NAKAYAMA Akinori *J*	KATO Sawao *J*	VORONIN Mikhail *U*
DDR	NAKAYAMA Akinori *J*	KASAMATSU Shigeru *J*	KENMOTSU Eizo *J*	TSUKAHARA Mitsuo *J*

WOMEN

Team	Individual	Floor	Vault	Bars
USSR	TOURISCHEVA Ludmila *U*	KORBUT Olga *U*	JANZ Karen *DDR*	JANZ Karen *DDR*
DDR	JANZ Karen *DDR*	TOURISCHEVA Ludmila *U*	ZUCHOLD Erika *DDR*	KORBUT Olga *U*
HUNGARY	LAZAKOVITCH Tamara *U*	LAZAKOVITCH Tamara *U*	TOURISCHEVA Ludmila *U*	ZUCHOLD Erika *DDR*

MONTREAL 1976
MEN

Team	Individual	Floor	Pommels	Rings
JAPAN	ANDRIANOV Nikolai *U*	ANDRIANOV Nikolai *U*	MAGYAR Zoltan *H*	ANDRIANOV Nikolai *U*
USSR	KATO Sawao *J*	MARCHENKO Vladimir *U*	KENMOTSU Eizo *J*	DETIATIN Alexandre *U*
DDR	TSUKAHARA Mitsuo *J*	KORMANN Peter *USA*	ANDRIANOV Nikolai *U*	GRECU Dan *R*

WOMEN

Team	Individual	Floor	Vault	Bars
USSR	COMANECI Nadia *R*	KIM Nelli *U*	KIM Nelli *U*	COMANECI Nadia *R*
RUMANIA	KIM Nelli *U*	TOURISCHEVA Ludmila *U*	TOURISCHEVA Ludmila *U*	UNGUREANU Teodora *R*
DDR	TOURISCHEVA Ludmila *U*	COMANECI Nadia *R*	DOMBECK Carola *DDR*	EGERVARI Marta *H*

Vault
AALTONEN Paavo *Fin*
ROVE Olavi *Fin.*
PATAKI Ferenc *H*
SOTORNIK L. *Cz*
MOGYOROSI-KLENCS J. *Hun*

P Bars
REUSCH M. *Sw*
HUHTANEN Vaikko *Fin*
[KIPFER C. *Sw*
[STALDER Joseph *Sw*

H Bar
STALDER Joseph *Sw*
LEHMANN Walter *Sw*
HUHTANEN Vaikko *Fin*

Vault
CHUKARIN Karl *U*
TAKEMOTO Masao *J*
ONO Tashashi *J*
VESAKO T. *J*

P Bars
EUGSTER Hans *Sw*
CHUKARIN Karl *U*
STALDER Joseph *Sw*

H Bar
GUNTHARD Jack *Sw*
STALDER Joseph *Sw*
SCHWARZMANN Alfred *G*

Beam
BOCHAROVA Nina *U*
GOROKHOVSKAYA Maria *U*
KORONDI Agnes *H*

---

ault
NTZ Helmut *G*
RATOV Valentin *U*
OV Yuri *U*

P Bars
CHUKARIN Victor *U*
KUBOTA Msami *J*
[TAKEMOTO Masao *J*
[ONO Takashi *J*

H Bar
ONO Takashi *J*
TITOV Yuri *U*
TAKEMOTO Masao *J*

m
YNINA Larissa *U*
NINA Tamara *U*
SKOVA E. *Cz*

---

lt
AKHLIN Boris *U*
O Takashi *J*
RTNOI Vladimir *U*

P Bars
SHAKHLIN Boris *U*
CARMINUCCI Giovanni *I*
ONO Takashi *J*

H Bar
ONO Takashi *J*
TAKEMOTO Masao *J*
SHAKHLIN Boris *U*

m
SOKOVA Eva *Cz*
YNINA Larissa *U*
RATOVA Sofia *U*

---

lt
MASHITA Haruhiro *J*
TSKI Victor *U*
NTAKARI Hannu *F*

P Bars
ENDO Yukio *J*
TSURUMI Shuji *J*
MENICHELLI Franco *I*

H Bar
SHAKHLIN Boris *U*
TITOV Yuri *U*
CERAR Miroslav *Y*

ult
SLAVSKA Vera *Cz*
TYNINA Larissa *U*
DOCHLA Birgit *G*

---

ult
RONIN Mikhail *U*
DO Yukio *J*
AMIDOV Serguei *U*

P Bars
NAKAYAMA Akinori *J*
VORONIN Mikhail *U*
KLIMENKO Victor *U*

H Bar
VORONIN Mikhail *U*
NAKAYAMA Akinori *J*
KENMOTSU Eizo *J*

am
ICHINSKAYA Natalia *U*
SLAVSKA Vera *Cz*
TRIK Larissa *U*

---

ult
STE Klaus *DDR*
IMENKO Victor *U*
NDRIANOV Nikolai *U*

P Bars
KATO Sawao *J*
KASAMATSU Shigeru *J*
KENMOTSU Eizo *J*

H Bar
TSUKAHARA Mitsuo *J*
KATO Sawao *J*
KASAMATSU Shigeru *J*

am
RBUT Olga *U*
ZAKOVITCH Ludmila *U*
JANZ Karen *DDR*

Vault
ANDRIANOV Nikolai *U*
TSUKAHARA Mitsuo *J*
KAJIYAMA Hiroshi *J*

P Bars
KATO Sawao *J*
ANDRIANOV Nikolai *U*
TSUKAHARA Mitsuo *J*

H Bar
TSUKAHARA Mitsuo *J*
KENMOTSU Eizo *J*
GIENGER Eberhard *BRD*

Beam
COMANECI Nadia *R*
KORBUT Olga *U*
UNGUREANU Teodora *R*

Above
Karen Janz took a bronze for the beam exercise in the Munich Olympic Games, but went on to win gold in vault and bars.

Above
Ludmila Tourischeva looks back on a career in which she won 10 gold, five silver and four bronze medals in World and Olympic championships.

Index

Acknowledgments

The publishers wish to thank the following individuals and organizations
for their kind permission to reproduce
the photographs in this book.
All Sport; 4-5, 8-9, 10, 11, 16, 18, 24, 25
above and below, 26-27, 28, 29, 30
above, 31, 34, 35 above, 36, 39 below
left and right, 40 below, 42-43, 45
below, 48, 49 above and below, 50 left,
50-51, 63, 67, 69 below, 70, 73 above, 75
above left, 76-77, (Tony Duffy)
Endpapers, 1, 37 below, 65 above; Alan
E Burrows; 6-7, 17, 19, 21, 22, 23, 30
left, 32-33, 35 below, 37 above, 38, 40
above, 41, 43 above and below, 44, 45
above, 46-47, 52-53, 54, 55, 56 above
left and right, 57 left and right, 58 left
and right, 59 above left, 62, 64, 65
below, 66, 69 above, 71, 72, 73 below,
74, 75 above right; Colorsport, 20, 68;
The Daily Telegraph Colour Library
(Waterman) 59 above right; Mary
Evans Picture Library, 14, 15 above
and below; Freelance Photographers
Guild — Alpha (Zimmerman) 60-61;
Michael Holford, 12, 13; The Image
Bank of Canada, 2-3;

Photography by Steve Powell (All
Sport) 78-87.

Our thanks also to: Jenny Wright,
Lionel Perry, Annie Horton, Ron Wat-
son and Noel Brett.

PDO 79-231